Foolish Church

Foolish Church

Messy, Raw, Real, and Making Room

to Marc

Lee Roorda Schott

Be foolish enough to love beyond walls

Lee Roorda Schott

CASCADE *Books* · Eugene, Oregon

FOOLISH CHURCH
Messy, Raw, Real, and Making Room

Copyright © 2019 Lee Roorda Schott. All rights reserved. Except for brief quotations in critical publications or reviews, no part of this book may be reproduced in any manner without prior written permission from the publisher. Write: Permissions, Wipf and Stock Publishers, 199 W. 8th Ave., Suite 3, Eugene, OR 97401.

Cascade Books
An Imprint of Wipf and Stock Publishers
199 W. 8th Ave., Suite 3
Eugene, OR 97401

www.wipfandstock.com

PAPERBACK ISBN: 978-1-5326-5327-8
HARDCOVER ISBN: 978-1-5326-5328-5
EBOOK ISBN: 978-1-5326-5329-2

Cataloguing-in-Publication data:

Names: Schott, Lee Roorda.
Title: Book title : Foolish church : messy, raw, real, and making room / Lee Roorda Schott.
Description: Eugene, OR: Cascade Books, 2019 | Includes bibliographical references.
Identifiers: ISBN 978-1-5326-5327-8 (paperback) | ISBN 978-1-5326-5328-5 (hardcover) | ISBN 978-1-5326-5329-2 (ebook)
Subjects: LCSH: Church work. | Prisoners—Religious life.
Classification: BV4465 .S67 2019 (paperback) | BV4465 (ebook)

Manufactured in the U.S.A.   02/01/19

For the women at the well
whose boundless love and wisdom
break down walls
including mine

For God's foolishness is wiser than human wisdom,
and God's weakness is stronger than human strength.

—1 CORINTHIANS 1:25

Contents

Permissions

Preface

1 Corinthians 1:18–31

One of the first times I shared the ideas in this book, a colleague stopped me cold with his response that amounted to *"What foolishness!"* I was describing the vision I felt God had planted in me, of churches out in the world offering a hearty welcome to women and men like the ones I meet in my ministry inside a prison. Of doors flung open to persons who sorely need the good news we hold inside our church walls, persons with mental illness, addiction, a history of incarceration, or sexual violence, or poverty. After I painted this picture, this colleague fixed me with an unswerving gaze and said, "Let me get this straight. We sent you to the prison to minister to those people so we wouldn't have to. And now you're gonna ask us to do it, out here, in our own churches?"

He had a point, of course; it's a ridiculous ask. It's not calculated to grow your giving. It might not help your attendance. It will definitely make some of your folks uncomfortable. To be *wise*, you might better look to the countless experienced leaders who will gladly advise you how to grow your church.

Before you read on, you might want to know I'm not wise like that. I once told a woman in prison that I forgave her, for her actions that had deeply injured me and our ministry there. I invited her to return to church, and she balked. "What if the others won't forgive me?" she asked; "what if they stay away because I'm there?" I said, "Even if that happens, you're still welcome." I leaned in and went on, "If it ends up that it's just the two of us sitting there praising God, there's still a place for you in the church." I meant it.

See, I'm always going to err on the side of making room. I have a hunch that when we make room for, well, *anyone*, we're going to end up needing to make room for the people who have been waiting for the church that matters, for the church that's willing to be The Church in all its fullness. That's the foolishness I've discovered inside a prison: When we're foolish enough to let church be messy, and real, and raw, we'll find ourselves making room in crazy beautiful ways, for unexpectedly beautiful people. That's what this book is about.

It took me awhile, in that early conversation with that shrewd colleague, to notice the dry humor behind what had felt like biting questions. It turned out he didn't mean to dissuade me, but to say *this is going to be hard.* He was right. It might turn out to be hard for you, too. You might call this some kind of foolishness!

But what if it's the kind of foolishness in which we might glimpse the wisdom of God? Go ahead. Read on.

Acknowledgments

Spending time as I do with women who feel alone in the world, stripped of every support and facing an uncertain future, I am acutely aware of the web of family, friends, churches, colleagues, and communities that have ever surrounded and buoyed me. The self that I am, and every bit of this book, are bathed in the love, hopes, correction, counsel, and generosity of more people than I can name here.

This book and any insights it contains are grounded in the good work and vision of those who started Women at the Well, the church inside the Iowa women's prison, including its inspiring first pastor, Arnette Pint. All of this has been possible by the huge *yes* we received from the warden Diann Wilder-Tomlinson in 2006, and the many smaller yeses and assistance supplied by Diann, her successors Patti Wachtendorf and Sheryl Dahm, our supervisors over the years—Robin Bagby, Paul Rode, and Courtney Arringdale—and countless other staff at the Iowa Correctional Institution for Women and the Iowa Department of Corrections.

So many women and men outside the prison have supported this congregation as leaders, volunteers, and donors. In recent years our council gave me room to pursue these ideas and time to write; you all made this book possible. As did Paul Witmer, who now graciously shares this ministry with me inside the prison. You who were part of the planning team for our Right Next Door conference in 2015 planted seeds that are reflected in this ongoing work.

I am not allowed to name you friends and sisters I have come to know inside the prison as the pastor of Women at the Well, but your faces and stories are woven into every page of this book. My words cannot begin to do justice to the richness of the life and ministry we've shared, but I hope you will find yourselves portrayed in these pages with the warmth and generosity I have intended. How many hurts and joys we have known together!

Acknowledgments

I must mention a few of you without whose encouragement and assistance this book would not have been written. Mary Mortenson caught this vision early on and kept me from shrinking back in a season when I had no energy to pursue it. Mike Malik (and Gracie) nurtured this work with space and hospitality for days on end, along with insightful and encouraging conversation. I am indebted to Debi, Connie, and Dara for direction at important moments, to Richard and Trish whose work inspires mine, and to Susan Galligan and Shari Miller who more than once reinforced my courage when I was faltering. My covenant group, my Courage and Renewal cohort, you twisted sisters, and the Prison and Jail Ministries group through the Disciples of Christ: you all had a hand in this writing.

My entire ministry, including this book, has been shaped by my friendship and much conversation with Cindy Hickman, who wisely advised me at a crucial point to clear the decks and do the writing. As did my husband Daniel; "Write the book!" you said, repeatedly. And so I have. You—along with our whole family—know better than anyone the sweat and tears that have accompanied this birthing; thank you for being at my side.

This text was strengthened by comments received from several friends mentioned above along with Martha Ward, Shannon Schott, Susan Vogel, Bill Mefford, Diane Olson-Schroeder, Mary Lautzenhiser Bellon, Janet Shaner, and Sue Owen-Anton. I am so grateful for the perspectives and insights you offered, grounded in your differing lives and experiences, and for your friendship that means so much to me. Thank you to Cascade and my editor Rodney Clapp, who have brought this work to fruition.

Finally, I want to thank you who will catch this vision and dare to be The Church in the ways you'll discover here. May we make room for those who look out at the world feeling alone, and help them know a different truth: *we are here together.*

Introduction

"I looked around myself and I realized I didn't know a single person who wasn't using meth." Carla was telling me what had led her to prison.[1] Her boyfriend had stayed away from meth for a whole year, because she insisted on it. But when he faced some reversals and said, "I'm sorry, I can't do this anymore," Carla wavered, and took stock of what was going on around her. Upon the unsettling realization that everyone in her life was already using meth, she gave in and joined him. "And ever since then," she said, "I've been trying to get back to my first high."

This happened in an Iowa community with dozens of churches, where two of my friends served well-meaning and lovely congregations, where hundreds of persons gather week after week to worship God and love their neighbors. But those neighbors evidently don't include the meth-using population. Most of those neatly dressed church people would probably say, "I don't know a single person who *does* use meth." How I wish Carla had known even one of them, that day she looked around.

I've been a "church person" my whole life. I love the church! I've been a member and leader of small churches and larger ones, sometimes rural and often suburban. I've laughed and cried and prayed earnestly with strangers who became family as we shared worship, choir, meetings, travels, tragedies, and joys. I've walked alongside beautiful souls as we have sought to follow Jesus Christ. As a forty-something second-career pastor, I thought I'd had a pretty good education in the richness that was *church*.

Then I went to prison, and I discovered church in a way I didn't realize I'd been missing.

---

1. I have substituted names for all the women whose stories I share in this book, except where full names are used, based on published news reports as indicated.

Prison was never in my plan. In this I am like the women who live there, except that it wasn't a judge that sent me to prison. A bishop did. In the United Methodist Church we clergy are appointed to the churches we serve. In 2011 the bishop sent me to serve as pastor to the church—Women at the Well United Methodist Church—inside the Iowa women's prison. I don't live there, but having spent (so far) seven years in this appointment, I have been "in prison" longer than many of the women in my charge.

Walking into the prison, I thought my role was to bring church to this population that desperately needed it. Little did I know *they* would show *me* church—a more raw, real church than I had ever known.

When you consider who gets sent to prison, it's no surprise that church feels raw there. The statistics tell a sobering story of who gets incarcerated in Iowa.[2]

More than 70 percent of our residents have a diagnosed mental illness. For some, her crime is integrally linked to voices she was hearing or to untreated psychosis. For many, prison life is complicated by medication changes, unhappy side effects, and repeated suicidal thoughts and even attempts. Her mental illness can interfere with relationships and participation in programs intended to help her, and it nearly always delays her release, as she waits for a bed at a facility that will take her. It breaks my heart when a woman weathering these storms tells me, "My parents don't think mental illness is even real."

Approximately 80 percent of our residents battle addiction. Many have been through one treatment program after another, with great hope that this time it will "take." The pull of addiction is very strong. Stacy sat with me not long before her release, saying, "I am done with meth. I'm gonna be with my kids again." Yet as we talked a cloud came across her face, and I watched her very present struggle. "I don't think I can stay away from using. I feel it in me; I still want it." A history of addiction has, too often, wrecked relationships with family and friends and taken away her sense of even who she is, separate from the needle or the bottle.

Ninety percent of the women incarcerated in Iowa are survivors of domestic violence and/or sexual assault (usually "and"). Pause for a moment and absorb that statement: *90 percent* of our state's incarcerated women

2. The statistics quoted here are based on reports from the Iowa Department of Corrections, conversations with staff members, and personal observations during seven years serving as pastor there.

were sexually victimized before they came to prison. That's practically everyone. It's a story repeated in so many conversations that it becomes almost matter-of-fact in the telling. The details start, too often, in childhood and nearly always include multiple encounters with many (usually) men, almost all of them family members or others well known to her. *Ninety percent.*

It's obvious from these numbers that many face more than one of these challenges. Experts say there is a delicate interconnection between addiction and mental illness; one can and often does lead to the other.[3] Further, the use of illicit substances is a common means of self-medicating the ongoing emotional trauma of sexual violence. One problem exacerbates the next, until—both in the deepening and the unwinding—it's hard to know where one begins and the other leaves off.

Given these statistics, it is unsurprising that many of these women have known poverty. In 2014 dollars, men and women nationwide heading for incarceration were earning less than $20,000 per year. That's 41 percent less than their counterparts who weren't going to prison. Women's numbers are even worse: women headed to prison were earning, on average, less than $15,000 per year.[4] These figures are interwoven with the mental illness, addiction, and sexual violence discussed above, and they both predict and reflect instability in employment, housing, transportation, and relationships.

In contrast, I live in the house where my grandmother was raised, on a farm owned by my family for more than a century. This land has been tilled by generations of relatives from my great-grandfather down to, now, my brother and my son. I've been married to the same man for nearly thirty-five years. I don't come from wealth, but there was always enough. I grew up with a supportive, intact, wide extended family that cheered for my smallest win. I never doubted that I could succeed in school, that I would go to college, and that I could pursue a career in law when that seemed the right path. Even my decision to leave that career to pursue a call to ministry was manageable given these long-standing advantages. I couldn't see how stable my life is until I began to learn the stories that accompany people into our justice system.

———

3. See, e.g., O'Leary, "Addiction and Mental Illness."
4. Rabuy and Kopf, "Prisons of Poverty."

While I was busy leaving my legal career, starting seminary, and beginning to serve as a student pastor, the groundwork was being laid for a church to be started at the Iowa women's prison. Numerous individuals, committees, and leaders in the Iowa United Methodist Church were pursuing conversations with the Iowa Correctional Institution for Women to see if this might be possible. This happened according to a model developed and promoted by Prison Congregations of America, which boasts more than thirty worshipping communities around the United States.[5] The first pastor, Arnette Pint, began serving in July 2006 and on February 8, 2007 Women at the Well was consecrated as a duly constituted church. While we are United Methodist in origin, our work is ecumenical in spirit, practice, and, increasingly, in support and connection.

In the years that followed, I came to know Women at the Well as a church like and unlike the ones many of us attend outside of prison walls. Like most churches, we worship every week, but our services are on Thursdays at 7 PM. This timing makes it possible for guests to visit from a church or community group—and they do, nearly every week, according to a calendar that fills up nearly a year in advance.[6] These guests go through a clearance process mandated by the prison and they enter through a metal detector. They walk up a hill to the building that houses our religious programs, which we call the Sacred Place.[7] They join in a worship service that feels familiar in ritual, yet heightened in emotion and engagement, and constrained by the rule that prohibits touch other than brief handshakes during the passing of the peace.

Having our services on Thursdays also makes me available on Sundays to share about Women at the Well in other churches' worship services. That calendar, too, fills early and I have spoken in dozens of local churches, small and large, accompanied by sunshine, rain, snow, and, once, a sparrow that flew through the wide-open doors of a small country chapel.

Like other churches, we do Christian education and outreach, and for each month our inside leadership group chooses missions that our residents' offerings will support—paid out of their earnings that have, during

5. See appendix A for a brief description of the PCA model of prison ministry and a link to their website.

6. At the time of publication, this privilege had been suspended. Perhaps you will pray with us for its restoration.

7. The word *chapel* is more exclusively Christian than the activities this building hosts, so we use the broader "Sacred Place" to encompass the breadth of religions accommodated there. My office—a small room formerly used for storage—is located there.

my time there, mostly ranged from twenty-four to sixty cents an hour.[8] We invest a lot of time in pastoral care. We sing, and pray, and lead the church together. Equally as important, we love, laugh, and weep together through the trials and joys that come with prison life.

In those years before I was appointed there, I didn't think Women at the Well had a lot to do with me. I was glad for the leaders who had the vision to get this church started; I was not among them. I was proud of Iowa United Methodists for daring to embrace this somewhat foolish project, but my interest was satisfied with an occasional visit to their worship with members of my church. In a moment of clarity when I felt God say to me, "You're gonna get asked to do this," to serve as pastor for Women at the Well, my heart sank. I decidedly did not want to go there. I couldn't know then what soon became true: that I would go there and be the pastor, and that I would love it, not least because I was about to discover a church more real than I could have imagined.

This introduction would be incomplete without naming some messy truths about our criminal justice system or—perhaps more correctly—our system of criminal *injustice*. The United States now incarcerates more people, and a higher percentage of our people, than any other country in the world,[9] even though this does not make us safer.[10] Lawyer and author Michelle Alexander has helped us see how this system of mass incarceration is fueled by historical and continuing racism embedded in systems of law-making, policing, adjudication, sentencing, and corrections.[11] Our culture is becoming more aware of the ways implicit bias sustains racial disparities even among those of us who sincerely believe in and want to support equality and justice.[12] These realities are entangled with many of the stories I share in this book, because they have created and they reinforce the often unjust structures within which these stories reside.

8. This practice, too, was suspended in late 2018 and we pray for its restoration.

9. BBC News, "World Prison Populations"; American Civil Liberties Union, "Mass Incarceration."

10. Head and Norquist, "The High Costs."

11. Alexander, *New Jim Crow*. See also Stevenson, *Just Mercy*.

12. A brief introduction to this idea and a link to the Harvard Implicit Bias Test can be found at Perception Institute, "Implicit Bias." Google has a training video for its employees on this subject, which can be extrapolated to other industries: https://www.youtube.com/watch?v=NW5s_-Nl3JE. For a more extended discussion of implicit bias, see Banaji and Greenwald, *Blindspot*.

Another raw truth of this book is that it comes from my experience of just one side of these stories. As pastor, I interact with incarcerated women who mostly manage to bring their best selves to their contact with me. I am shielded from their less guarded moments and the many daily decisions that relate to security and order within the prison. No wonder I was surprised when, for instance, one of the seemingly gentle women I describe in this book showed up on a training video, committing an assault on another resident!

Further, I am neither required nor allowed to face my congregants' victims or family members, some of whom would surely recoil when I describe how precious and dear these women have become to me. In day-to-day contact, I can almost forget that these sisters have been judged by our legal system to have broken the law, and that most are there because of some illicit action they chose.[13] As we embark together on this book that invites you to remember the humanity we share with persons we have overlooked, we must not ignore the wounds that persist within the communities affected by persons' wrongs. I hope that even those who have been horrendously victimized can agree that our communities become safer when perpetrators become more whole, grounded, and faithful.

This is not a book about prison ministry. I hope it will be interesting to you who are doing ministry inside a prison or jail. But this is a book about ministry, period. About The Church, period. By "The Church" I mean church as it's meant to be, when we are most fully who we're called to be, living out with passion and faithfulness the work God has entrusted to us. The goal of this book is to share what I have learned of The Church through this most unlikely setting, in order to help us be more fully who we're called to be in every place. I want us churches to live out our mission of connecting with the people who are right next door in our communities but often separate or hidden—even in our pews!—because the less respectable parts of our experiences are often not welcomed inside our doors.

This book shares lessons I have learned as a pastor behind bars, things this "church person" didn't know when she arrived in prison. In each case, I share stories that characterize that particular learning, and I seek to draw connections between what I have discovered and how it is different from

13. I say "most" because some are guilty only of being in the wrong place at the wrong time, often with the wrong person. Bryan Stevenson helps to illumine the limitations of our judicial decisions in his book *Just Mercy*. Also, see Schwartzapfel and Levintova, "How Many Innocent People."

the experience I've generally had in churches outside. I close each chapter with specific actions and then questions to guide your reflection and, I hope, conversation with your church leadership, missions, outreach, or care teams.

It might be easier *not* to have those conversations. Some of them will be unsettling. Pretty soon you could find yourself drawn into places you would have avoided, and you might begin to love some of the people you meet there. I know something about this foolishness; don't say I didn't warn you!

But then again: aren't we called to make room?

1

The Church Doesn't Need Us
to Hide Our Scars

Is there anyone that fails? Is there anyone that falls?
Am I the only one in church today, feelin' so small?
'Cause when I take a look around ev'rybody seems so strong
I know they'll soon discover that I don't belong

—MARK HALL AND NICHOLE NORDEMAN[1]

When Meagan was getting ready to leave prison, she was excited to go and live with her grandmother. One among many reasons was the addiction recovery ministry at her grandmother's church. Meagan had participated in it before and knew what a good program it was. She was startled when Grandma let Meagan know she must not say anything about having been in prison. Grandma was glad for her granddaughter to join in the recovery ministry, but Meagan must never reveal the secret of her incarceration. Meagan came to talk about this, bewildered. "How do I participate if I can't talk about my *stuff*?"

The scar of a prison stay was embarrassing for Meagan's grandmother. Clearly, she had hidden this part of her story from her friends at church.

---

1. Hall and Nordeman, "Stained Glass Masquerade."

She must have sensed that there was a line there, one that she could not cross.

If we have been part of a church, we likely have an implicit sense of its lines, between scars that can and cannot be shared. Addiction falls on one side in that church, at least for Meagan's grandmother; it can be spoken. Incarceration falls on the other; a prison stay is a scar that must be kept hidden. In another church, the line might put both addiction and incarceration on the must-be-hidden side.

It's worth wondering where that line falls in our own churches. What do you hide? What prayers can you say out loud, and which ones do you hold back? I remember a mother, Penny, at the church we attended decades ago, asking prayers for her daughter who had been arrested. That I remember this exposes the line that renders incarceration unspeakable in many churches. In all my years attending worship, I don't remember a similar prayer request for a close friend or family member affected by incarceration—other than the prayers I voice when I now visit a church! It's not that Penny was the only parent, grandparent, sibling, or friend who had such a need; it's that she was peculiar in daring to cross that very evident line.

We hold a lot back. We sit in rows looking pretty respectable most of the time. Scars are not the first thing you notice when you walk into most churches.

When people come to worship with Women at the Well, they cross a lot of lines, expecting scars. I hear it from the guests who join us that Thursday night, and from residents who have just arrived. They know the space they're entering.

Among the residents present, week by week, the scars are of diverse origin. We welcome "lifers" who were convicted of murder. They sit next to women incarcerated for nonviolent drug offenses or driving under the influence. There are women who used to care for children whose injuries were attributed to her wrongdoing or carelessness. Down the row will be a woman sentenced for a sex offense. Often crimes like arson, prostitution, theft, embezzlement, and assault are represented in that room.

The differences among charges and individual circumstances are obscured by their presence here, wearing prison-issue blues and grays, each with a plastic badge that bears her name, photo, and seven-digit offender number. The visible details try to contain her life story in this one fact:

she's in prison. Her scars include arrest, charges, conviction, and sentencing. What else could we need to know?[2]

In many churches, one could almost think there's nothing *to* know about the decently dressed, well behaved people we'll meet there. Nothing unsavory, anyway. No scars. We come into the church with our act together and our story straight, ready to present our best selves to God. Our conduct is bounded by an unspoken compact that assumes we are generally good people who will behave with decorum and restraint—perhaps especially in the white, Protestant, Midwestern churches I have known best. At some level every church has its version of these limits.

Our unstated agreement gives us a little room to be imperfect. We might giggle together at the brightly dressed children who innocently do the unexpected. We'll share knowing glances when Grandpa dozes off during the sermon and jolts awake at his own snoring. There can be gasps and a few tears at unexpected news of health issues and hospitalizations, and we can trust that these needs will be met with empathy and support. Broken limbs, hip and knee replacement, pneumonia, back problems, cancer: these are the staples of congregational prayer requests. Hospital stays and convalescence generate creative ideas about how the community might care for the family. Within the twenty-four hours after my middle son was born unable to breathe on his own, members of our church family were providing child care for our oldest, shoveling the snow from our driveway, and setting up a schedule for meals delivered graciously to our home.

Our tacit understanding does include some limits on what can be shared and answered. Certain diseases have carried shame: leprosy, tuberculosis, cancer, and HIV/AIDS.[3] Over time, cancer has mostly shed its stigma to become a commonly voiced prayer concern. Still, I noticed a conditional response to my mother as she developed and died of lung cancer; my mention of her disease was often met with edgy silence. "She isn't a smoker," I'd hurry to add, answering the unspoken question. Would the response have been less generous if I'd said "a pack a day for forty years"? *Should* our care depend on that answer?

---

2. Our current prison administration has loosened the rules to allow T-shirts in various colors. On a recent Thursday, someone remarked with delight that our choir "looked like Easter eggs," because of the many pastel shirts worn by our members!

3. Sontag, "Disease as Political Metaphor"; Mukherjee, *Emperor of All Maladies*, 37–38, 181, 315–16.

Mental illness is another condition that is rarely named out loud. A new diagnosis of depression, bipolar, or other mental condition involves us in medications, changed expectations, and next steps in much the same way as my own recent diagnosis of diabetes. Yet we have responded to *mental* illness as if it's different and thus harder to mention in most churches. It's more fearsome. A disease that can affect our thinking and our perceptions generates different worries, and thus it carries a more pronounced scar, at least in our collective imagination.[4]

Upon a diagnosis that we are able to share, and if an illness culminates in the death of a loved one, there will be generous support. But even then it's worth noting the boundaries within which our responses are expected to fall. Self-control is lifted up. Uncontrolled sobbing is rarely heard. It saddens me how little space we allow in our culture—including in our churches—for grief to be expressed. "I'm doing pretty well today," said my neighbor, just days after her husband died. "I haven't cried all morning." As if one can earn points by holding back tears! Sadly, given the narrow emotional range of many churches, she probably does.

When someone's behavior falls outside the bounds of perceived propriety, church people know how to let her know she's broken the unstated covenant. It happens in every church, through collectively averted eyes or the stage whisper meant to be overheard. Women I meet in prison are more open than most in recounting times they received those messages. Brooke told me she found that her long-time church could no longer welcome her once she became an addict. "I was not wanted the way I was, because I made the choice to use. It was made pretty clear to me: *you* did this, so you could change it. But I didn't." Ginger described a similar experience with the church of her youth, where she had been a regular participant in mission trips, service projects, and weekly worship. "Do they know you're here?" I asked, when she wanted help finding a church that would welcome her when she returned home. "No, as soon as I started getting in trouble, they cut me off," she said. "I'd never go back there."

Many women I meet in prison, when they describe their early faith experiences, mention *tights*. They don't describe unconditional welcome or spiritual awakening. They remember *tights*, as in those stretchy, constricting nylons pulled onto little girls' legs. It should give us pause that many women's most vivid memories of church are the tights they wore as

---

4. A brief introduction to the issue of stigma as it relates to mental illness, with a quiz and a pledge to help reduce stigma, can be found at NAMI, "StigmaFree."

girls. Tights are a rigid marker of being "dressed up" and therefore good enough—uncomfortable enough!—for church. Ask any woman of a certain age; we remember how relentlessly the tights would slip down or bind or, heaven forbid, get snagged. That memory of tights seems an apt metaphor for the dressed-up, constricted experience church has been for far too many people.

One of our leaders inside the prison, Connie, once described prison as a place where "we know we're broken." It's a truth that, for many women, brings freedom. They don't have to hide anymore, which is a relief for those who have hidden, most of their lives. She gets to bring her whole self. And she gets to be part of a community of people doing the same thing. It's the opposite of *tights*; here we *loosen*.

This means I have a lot of conversations that go deep, faster than I would have imagined. The filter that makes many of us reticent to speak of our deepest wounds feels mostly inoperative inside the razor wire. I barely knew Danielle when she told me about her abortion. One of the first things I knew about Marissa was that, during her recent year outside prison, she had attempted suicide four times. Desiree told me about her son born of rape; Krista shared her struggle with gender identity; Stacy said quite openly that she would probably return to prostitution after she left prison. Countless women admit they're mad at God.

What gets said so openly can become a starting point for further conversation, prayer, and healing. Sometimes just putting it into words seems to be enough. One day I sat with a woman I had never met, who tearfully let loose a long story of challenges, losses, and hurts. When she fell silent, I felt mute. What could I say in response to all this pain? I stammered out some halting words to that effect and was astonished when she looked at me, visibly heartened, and said, "That's OK. I needed to talk. I feel better. Thanks for listening."

Something important happens when we shed the *tights*.

The trouble with lines and tights is that we have to contort ourselves to fit into them. We'll hide our tears and do our sobbing in private, or skip church when we feel like we might lose control. We won't talk about the disease that feels like it's our own fault, or that's too complicated for the community; they're probably busy already, taking casseroles to that family with a more socially acceptable problem.

We hide a lot of scars behind problems that *can* be spoken. I remember an adult Sunday school lesson on sin, in a suburban church where the leader said God had told him to stop driving over the speed limit. Speeding is, Robert said, breaking the law, and therefore a sin. As a dedicated "nine-over" driver, I felt relieved that God hadn't been talking to *me* about that particular transgression! In retrospect, I wonder how long it took Robert to decide that speeding was a sin he could reasonably mention. Could he have talked instead about lust? Or an ethical compromise he had just made at work? We censor our examples to fit the unsaid rules.

Another Sunday school class outside the prison had an earnest conversation about God helping in the hard moments of life. Asked for a real-life example, one woman volunteered her story of her car breaking down by the side of the road. As the conversation unfolded, we learned it was a late-model sedan, on a busy suburban street not far from the church, in broad daylight, and help arrived within thirty minutes. I have no doubt this experience was stressful for this aging woman, and she saw God in the midst of it. But I have to believe that many harder, deeper stories were represented in that room, longing—or perhaps fearing—to be told.

Teachings on church growth and evangelism reinforce this sense that our scars aren't really welcome. Articles focus on vibrant young people, smiling children, and intact families. That's who we want to come into our doors. No one says their target market is "people who are tempted to use meth" or "families reeling from domestic violence."

Some of us will remember "Saddleback Sam," a profile created in the mid-1990s to describe the evangelistic target for Rick Warren's church, Saddleback, in southern California.[5] Saddleback Sam is a typical unchurched man, late thirties or early forties, with a college degree and a professional or entrepreneurial career. He's self-satisfied, places a priority on fitness, has an unlisted phone number, and lives in a gated community with his wife, Saddleback Samantha.[6] Warren said the Saddleback Sam profile was well known within that church, and discussed "in detail in every membership class."[7]

---

5. Warren, *Purpose-Driven Church*, 169. Warren is better known for his book *A Purpose-Driven Life*.

6. Warren, *Purpose-Driven Church*, 169–70. I've always thought that in a less patriarchal world, they would together have been the target, rather than Samantha just being along for the ride. Today I'm aware that even that critique suffers from heteronormativity.

7. Ibid., 169.

There's the rub: What happens to people that don't fit the profile? What if that fine home is one paycheck away from foreclosure, or their story includes addiction, violence, or a parent with mental illness? Will it be safe for them to even show that side of themselves? And what about the others who come—Saddleback Jose, Saddleback Sadeisha, Irvine Irma? Surely the church will welcome them, but won't those outliers eventually figure out that they are *not* who the church was hoping to welcome?[8] Sure, they can pick up the crumbs left over from Sam's table, but is that space really *for* them?

When we can bring our whole selves to church, scars and all, we free up a lot of energy we were using to keep those scars hidden. We might begin to uncover other wounds that need to be aired. Imagine using our energy not to hold ourselves together, but to become well!

It's what I saw Alexis do, working through a study on forgiveness.[9] As she focused on forgiveness in one area of her life, other issues surfaced. On one clear-sighted day, she came to recall some times when her husband had shoved her, coming after her even when she fled to a different room. Up until that moment, she would have described her marriage as *complicated*, but she didn't know it had been *abusive*. I don't believe she was trying to cover up this scar. *She didn't know it was there.* Even in a setting where nearly all—*90 percent*—bear this particular scar, it was a long time before Alexis could see it in her own story.

One day Tamara came to me and said, "I want you to know, Pastor Lee, that I finally was able to tell the truth." She explained that she had always maintained she didn't do the thing she was in prison for. "I finally was able to say yes, I did it." It was no coincidence that this happened just days after Tamara had stood in front of the church to renew her baptism. Together with a dozen friends, she professed her faith, agreeing through the words of our baptismal ritual to "renounce the spiritual forces of wickedness"

8. The Saddleback Church website today says they're a place where "the depressed, the hurting, and hopeless can come and find help." "I'm New Here," Saddleback Church, http://saddleback.com/visit/about/new-here. Even the 1995 book explains that, as the church grew, they added "additional ministries and outreach programs to reach young adults, single adults, prisoners, the elderly, parents with ADD children, and Spanish-, Vietnamese- and Korean-speaking people, as well as many other targets." Warren, *Purpose-Driven Church*, 160.

9. We have made repeated use of an online "Forgiveness Challenge" based on *The Book of Forgiving* by Desmond Tutu and Mpho Tutu. The online study is accessible in both seven- and thirty-day versions: https://www.forgivenesschallenge.com/.

and to "resist evil, injustice, and oppression in whatever forms they present themselves."[10] It is also noteworthy that the person to whom Tamara first told the truth was another member of Women at the Well's leadership group. There's strength in a church that can face one another's scars and still offer love and support.

I am grateful that this happened for Tamara. She had been in prison for four years. That's four years of looking in the mirror and seeing only very dimly. It's four years of hiding. Tamara came to the truth a few months before she would leave prison. I'm glad she could leave able to face this scar.

Why is it so hard for this to happen, out in the world? What gets in the way of us being able to bring our whole selves to church, scars and all?

We have come to believe this is the way it's *supposed* to be. The church isn't supposed to be messy; wisdom says it's supposed to hold good people, holy folk. We might laugh a bit at that caricature and admit that we don't totally fit the stereotype. But many of us have that expectation. We want good role models and safe settings for our children.[11] We want the church to be a place of calm and rest. Scars don't fit into that ideal.

We could even find biblical support for this position. The Bible, in too many places, seems to lift up "us" good people who are encouraged to distance ourselves from "those people" who are scarred. I see it repeatedly in the Psalms.[12] Psalm 26 is unequivocal:

> I do not sit with the worthless,
> nor do I consort with hypocrites;
> I hate the company of evildoers,
> and will not sit with the wicked (Ps 26:4–5).

Even Jesus, in the New Testament, is not above distinctions like these.[13] When a Canaanite woman asks him in Matthew 15 to heal her daughter, Je-

---

10. These words are from the United Methodist baptismal liturgy, relevant portions of which can be found at appendix 2.

11. We'll talk in chapter 4 about boundaries and the reasonable expectation of safety when we go to church.

12. See Pss 101; 119:158; 139:19–22; 140; 141.

13. In Matthew 7, Jesus urges, "Beware of false prophets" who will be known by their fruits, and those bearing bad fruit will be "cut down and thrown into the fire" (7:15, 20); see also Matt 12:30–37. In Matthew 13, Jesus gives us the parable of the good and bad seed, with the promise that all who cause sin and do evil will be thrown "into the furnace of fire, where there will be weeping and gnashing of teeth" (13:42); see also Matthew 13:47–50 and Matthew 25:31–46. In Matthew 23 Jesus rails against the religious leaders,

sus refuses. "I came only for my own people," he says, referring to the Jews, who were distinct from her people. When she kneels right in front of him and pleads for help, he responds with a slur (Matt 15:22–26).[14] Although he relents upon the woman's third appeal (Matt 15:27–28), the sting of his initial reaction lingers.

But the witness of the gospel overall does not honor lines like these. Jesus went where the sinners are. He let an unclean woman touch his cloak and receive healing (Mark 5:25–34). He surprised everyone when he singled out the tax collector Zacchaeus and invited himself to his home (Luke 19:1–10). If Jesus came today, I have no doubt we would find him outside most of our churches, with *those people* that we might not have welcomed. It's simply not Christ-like for our churches to have an admission standard based on purity and decorum.

It is through that lens that I read words like those quoted above from Psalm 26. I have no doubt that the psalmist wants me to avoid the people these words describe. But I have come to see it entirely differently. *I do not sit with the worthless,* I think, *because not a single person I've met is worthless.* Nor, indeed, are they hypocrites, evildoers, or wicked. This is not to say that hypocrisy, evil, and wickedness are not real. But those things are never the whole story. Every evil in this world is done by a living, breathing, precious child of God. Every one of us can be transformed. Renewed.

Another reason we'd rather have a scar-free church is that it seems simpler. If people bare their scars, it will demand something of us. We won't be able to just sit next to that person and then go about our day; we'll have to make room for their problems and perhaps do something to help.

There's truth there. Many of us have surely found ourselves in a situation where we tried to help, just a little, and soon found ourselves overwhelmed, frustrated, and manipulated. We'll talk in chapter 4 about how good boundaries can keep all parties healthy in those situations.

Even so, is it not the work of our churches to make room for one another? The Apostle Paul used the metaphor of the body of Christ to remind of us of how interconnected we are. "If one member [of the body] suffers,

---

repeatedly calling them "hypocrites" and "blind guides" (23:23–24, 27, 29) and even "snakes" and "brood of vipers" (23:33–34).

14. When Jesus says, "It is not fair to take the children's food and throw it to the dogs" (15:26), he is using a "deeply offensive [image] of unworthy or hostile outsiders" that is foreshadowed in Matthew 7:6. Coogan, ed., *New Oxford Annotated Bible,* Matt 7:6n.

all suffer together with it; if one member is honored, all rejoice together with it" (1 Cor 12:26).

We could worry that we can't handle all those scars. The unveiling of their hurt might unearth ours. How much better to keep pain at a distance, where it seems like it can be controlled! So long as scars are only occasionally visible, we can think that they happen only to other people, and we might even convince ourselves that those people bear the blame for what happened. We would rather not face into the ways that life is unfair and justice incomplete. If we are brought face to face with the truth that scars are all around us—even *in us*—the world must be unsafe, and our mechanisms for comfort and security unveiled as illusions.

Not to mention that the baring of scars—theirs and ours—could leave us sad and joyless. Pretty soon we'll find ourselves with a bunch of wailing and sobbing people, and who wants that? Won't we all be more comfortable if we keep as much of this hidden as possible?

Concerns like these keep some people from coming inside the prison as guests in our worship services: It's going to be too raw. I don't want to get that close. We've sent our scarred people away so we wouldn't have to see them; why would we want to go there? It is one of the great mysteries of worship at the prison that these worries seem unfounded. You'd think if everyone knows we're all scarred, and tears are welcomed, our time together would be grim indeed. It isn't.

Most weeks we welcome as many as ten guests, who sit next to residents and begin to hear the stories the prison holds. As a resident's story unfolds, she who was supposed to fit neatly into very limiting categories no longer does. She becomes a living, breathing human being with hopes and hurts, dreams and hurdles. She begins to matter, personally, in a way none of us—not even she!—thought possible.

After worship, which always includes Holy Communion, we spend a few minutes with that week's outside guests debriefing and answering questions. I'll ask, "What did you notice? What surprised you?" Week after week someone will say, surprised, "They're just like us!" Our guests arrive expecting to meet scary outlaws and instead they meet human beings who remind them of their niece, their long-time friend, or the neighbor who lives down the block. Nearly always someone will notice the eagerness, the joy with which our residents gather for worship. This is no gloomy cry-fest, even if some weep. It is a gathering of real people who bring all that they are, their whole selves, with tears and laughter, scars and beauty, their uniqueness as well as their common humanity. Looking down those rows, we realize we're seeing beautiful, amazing children of God.

As the Apostle Paul said, "God chose what is foolish in the world to shame the wise; God chose what is weak in the world to shame the strong" (1 Cor 1:27). Worshiping with our sisters at Women at the Well challenges every designation of "foolish" or "weak" with which we entered.

The Nigerian girl Little Bee, in the book by that name, expresses something of this. She says,

> I ask you right here please to agree with me that a scar is never ugly. That is what the scar makers want us to think. But you and I, we must make an agreement to defy them. We must see all scars as beauty. Okay? This will be our secret. Because take it from me, a scar does not form on the dying. A scar means, *I survived*.[15]

Little Bee had witnessed enough horrors to speak with authority about dying and survival, and the conditions under which scars form. My sisters in prison are, sadly, similarly wise, and have taught me these same truths.

We get to bring our whole selves to church.

So how do we become churches that don't need people to hide their scars?

We bare some of our scars. I'm not suggesting that we spew out all the deepest, darkest secrets of our lives. It's not healthy for us to work out our unhealed pain, in public, in front of everyone. Many of us have found ourselves shifting uncomfortably in our seats when a leader spoke long and heatedly about something she clearly still needed to work through. I'm not advocating that we do all of that work publicly; we don't need to inflict our unresolved woundedness on the community that surrounds us.

Still, we can look long and hard at those lines we started with and wonder how we could move them a bit, with even our own witness, in our own church. If the line says you can have an earring but not a tattoo, why not wear a sleeveless shirt that bares that rose, or skull, that you've always kept concealed on your upper arm, and maybe tell the story of why you put

---

15. Cleave, *Little Bee*, 9 (emphasis in original).

it there? If the line says you can share about losing your job but not about the foreclosure on your home, could you dare to tell the rest of that story?

If the line says you can talk about a birth defect but not a mental illness, why not share about your own experiences? Most of us have personal stories that relate to mental health; mental illness would carry less stigma if those stories were told more freely. I shared this idea over coffee with a talented church friend. He lowered his voice as he told me about his own mental illness, which started in his teens. "People were ugly about it," he said. It's well controlled now, but "I've never talked about it publicly." Could we dare to move that line? This is a question for every member of a church, every clergy leader and every layperson. How can we move the line by sharing our own scars?

Remember, our stories are our own to tell. We have to decide what we are willing to say, knowing that we won't control what happens next. Paige said in grief group, which had an expectation of confidentiality, that she was HIV positive. She was understandably angry when Tiffany broke the group's rules to blab that secret around the prison yard. It was a reminder that, once we tell our secrets, we no longer control them.

We don't flinch when others bare their scars. I have learned that the first gift I can give a woman at the prison is to let her tell her story, in all its beauty and in all its brokenness, and I won't flinch. I may not love what I hear. There may be room, later, to push toward greater honesty in this narrative where truth feels distant. I may need to turn my attention elsewhere if she lingers in that victim or martyr stance without moving toward healing. But my first reaction must be unflinching openness, or else I risk forfeiting any chance I have to be present in her life.

I've had people tell me about suicide attempts, how they harmed a child, how they're hoping to get revenge on someone. I've learned to listen and pray and ask for God to give me strength and direction. After they leave I might go and wash my hands with hot, soapy water, a ritual of washing away the pain I find myself holding.[16] But I need to make it OK for the conversation to happen: for her to share her truth, to ask for forgiveness, to process her thinking, to wonder what the future looks like, or whatever she needs. Aware of her own scars, she's already worried that she's beyond the bounds of what is acceptable and reasonable. We help her accept herself

16. I am indebted to a woman at Prairiewoods Franciscan Spirituality Center in Hiawatha, Iowa who commended this practice.

and move forward when we listen without turning away. As the Quaker teacher and author Parker Palmer puts it,"We stand with simple attentiveness at the borders of [her] solitude—trusting" that will help her employ the resources she already has.[17]

This is not some remarkable pastoral practice. It's the simple practice of compassionate humanity. Along the way we realize we receive as much as we give: It is an exquisite gift when another human being entrusts us with her truth. Let us hold it ever so gently.

We don't let scars define one another. If we allow people to see our scars, we run the very real risk that they will no longer see anything else about us. If we let a person's scar define her, then we—and others—will learn that it's not a safe place for scars to be seen. Returning to prison after months at home, Stephanie told me how completely she had felt defined by her prior incarceration. She would become overwhelmed at family gatherings where person after person engaged her in the same conversation: How is your sobriety going? How are you staying clean? What is working for you in recovery? "There are so many other things I want to talk about," Stephanie said to me. "My career, my dog, my apartment. But they look at me and all they can see is prison."

In John 9, Jesus healed a man who had been born blind. This man had for many years sat, day after day, at the side of the road in his village, begging. After his healing, his neighbors fell into an argument about whether this seeing man before them was that same man (John 9:8–9). For all those years, his identity had been *blind beggar*. When healing changed both parts of that identity, they couldn't recognize him. All they had ever seen of him was something that he no longer was!

Any known scar can overtake our identity. We become that thing that people see. It begins to be all *we* can see of ourselves, too. One could conclude that Meagan's grandma was right, and if we want to be free of the scar of incarceration, or any other scar, we must keep it hidden. "Whatever happens, don't let people know," Grandma might say. "You don't want to be defined that way."

There's a better answer. It has to do with *relationship*. The more fully engaged we are in relationship with one another, the more we'll know one another's scars, and the less they'll define us. We'll talk more about that in chapter 2.

17. Palmer, *Hidden Wholeness*, 64.

[Jesus] said to him the third time, "Simon son of John, do you love me?" Peter felt hurt because he said to him the third time, "Do you love me?" And he said to him, "Lord, you know everything; you know that I love you." Jesus said to him, "Feed my sheep." (John 21:17)

When the risen Christ meets Peter on the shore, their reunion is burdened by Peter's deep wound: he had denied knowing Jesus in those blurred hours after Jesus' arrest. Three times, Peter denied Jesus, just as Jesus had predicted (John 18:15–18, 25–27). Far earlier, Jesus had said Peter was the rock on which he would build the church (Matt 16:17–18)! Peter's mistake seems to set that plan adrift.

When Jesus pursues a conversation with Peter by the sea, Jesus neither ignores Peter's mistakes nor shames him for them. Instead, he asks Peter three times, "Do you love me?" Here are three chances for Peter to *claim* Jesus, symbolically undoing his threefold denial, making it possible for this wound to heal. The third time, Peter cries out, "Lord, you know everything!" Yes, he does! And that's the point: Even knowing everything, Jesus replies, "Feed my sheep."

Peter's wound healed but it left a scar that must have affected his ensuing ministry. It is part of the "everything" about Peter that Jesus knew and invited into ministry anyway. All of us come scarred into the work Jesus has for us. Still Jesus says to us, "Feed my sheep."

Questions:

a. What are some of the "scars" that are visible among the people in your church? How did those come to be revealed? How were those individuals received? Was it safe for them when issues became known? Did they feel supported in dealing with those matters? Ask them!

b. What "scars" can be safely shared in your church? (Your church's prayer list may be a good place to see this.) Are some wounds too deep? Too shameful?

c. Think about the scars you bear personally. Is your church a safe place to share about them? How do you know what is or is not safe to share?

d. How is a church strengthened when persons feel they can share about their deepest wounds? What need is served when brokenness is kept hidden? Is it worth it?

e. Name one or two specific steps you can take to make your church more open to telling the truth of its people's brokenness. (Hint: A good starting point may be *you* telling some of your truth.)

2

The Church Is More about Relationships Than Programs

Blest be the tie that binds
our hearts in Christian love;
the fellowship of kindred minds
is like to that above.

—JOHN FAWCETT[1]

The afternoon I met Terri, she was at the end of her rope. She came unannounced and asked if we could talk. I came around my desk and she sat down next to me, undone. Her unkempt hair fell this way and that as her head and body rocked in a perpetual motion that I knew was related to mental illness. She barely looked at me as she poured out a long story of addiction, abuse, bipolar disorder, and depression. She described stays in various institutions and multiple returns to prison. Her breathless flow of words was punctuated by tears that she dashed hastily away. She told of the family members who had cut her off and the bridges she had burned. "After everything I've done," Terri said, "no one wants to be near me anymore. Not one person."

1. "Blest Be the Tie that Binds," reprinted in United Methodist Publishing House, *United Methodist Hymnal*, 557.

There was a moment's pause as she gathered herself to continue, and I seized it. "Terri," I said. "I really want you to hear this." For the first time since she had entered, she sat stock still and listened. I looked her full in the face and said, "I'm really glad to be here with you right now." I meant it. "There's no place I'd rather be than having this conversation with you."

It surprises me that I could say those words, and know that they were true. They were possible only because I met Terri in the context of church. This is the place, after all, where we hear Jesus' parting commandment to "love one another" (John 13:34). Jesus calls those words a "new commandment," which always startles me. Love is the old, old story that permeates the Bible from its earliest pages! How can he call love "new," in his final words to his disciples?

It's because love has never become our normal response to other human beings. If I had met Terri out on the sidewalk, out in the world, or if I had noticed her at an adjoining table at a neighborhood restaurant, I wouldn't have loved her. I might have wished her away, uncomfortable at her behavior. I would have removed myself from her presence, certain that she could have nothing to do with my life.

My life has been enriched by the privilege of knowing Terri, and being her pastor. This relationship has made a difference in her life, too. My experience with Terri is for me a witness to the lesson that real relationship with real human beings is the first and best thing we do as a church.

If you were to look at many churches' newsletters and websites, you might think the most important thing is our *programs*. We announce this study or that mission trip. We schedule Vacation Bible School and our annual noodle dinner or all-church bazaar. Our calendar has entries for the women's group, the men's group, the singles' group, the youth group, the prayer group, the garden club, the seekers' group, and so on. All this before we even mention the committees that keep all of this going, and the praise team, choir, altar guild, usher corps, and hospitality group that contribute to our most prominent weekly activity: worship.

Early in my ministry serving a church in a small town, we had a planning conversation in which we embraced a vision of activities every night of the week, with lots of people coming in and out of our building. Over a few years, we lived that out; we became a church that had something happening most nights. During that time, we happily grew from what some would have called a pastor-sized church into a program-sized church.[2] That nomenclature was never meant to convey that the church was *about* pastor or programs; it had to do with how a church and its leadership function at different sizes. But there is a way that the growth of programs and committees puts a priority on administration. Maintaining a calendar full of programs can obscure the purpose behind them.

As our church grew, and we gathered in different configurations night after night, we built a lot of relationships. Our work together, including the administrative work of the church, is an important way that we build community with one another. But along the way, some of us burned out. The meetings didn't always get us closer to God and closer to one another.

I'm not the first to call out this concern. Many writers have urged churches to reclaim our priorities and not be carried along by programs.[3] I agree with their concerns but want to push further than many do toward *relationship* as the antidote.

When I started serving as a pastor inside the prison, I was promptly told what I could and couldn't offer to the women in my congregation. I can't call a family member on their behalf, or pass any message between people inside and outside the prison. I can't offer input on parole board decisions. I'm not allowed to write a job recommendation. I must not arrange for money to be given to any person. I can't give someone a note pad or a sparkly pencil, or even share a snack.

I felt cut off at the knees by these limits. I had come into ministry certain that part of my role was to offer *resources*. In fact, my pastoral care class in seminary had us develop a list of numbers to call when people came with foreseeable needs: addiction, domestic violence, mental illness, marriage conflict, and the like. Oh, you need money? Here's a list of local resources to call, or here might be a check from our pastor's discretionary fund. Or, sure, we'll ask the church for help after that fire that destroyed so many of your things. Oh, you need a counselor? Let me give you a referral to this counseling center. Oh, you're having problems with an alcoholic daughter? Here, you should connect her with AA[4] —and don't forget that Al-Anon

2. Mann, *Raising the Roof*, 7.

3. Rainer and Geiger, *Simple Church*, 4–8, 14; Warren, *Purpose-Driven Church*, 79; Wilson, "Underprogram Your Church."

4. "AA" refers to Alcoholics Anonymous; learn more at https://www.aa.org/.

might be a great resource for the rest of your family.[5] Looking back, I can see I went into "helping" mode, making sure no one left our conversation without a phone number and some concrete assistance.

But inside the prison, every one of those avenues of helping was blocked. It became very obvious, very quickly, that I really had just one thing to offer: my presence. I had *time*. I could listen, and ask questions, and do a little bit of talking myself. Oh—and I'm allowed to have a box of really good tissues at the ready. I buy the soft ones, with lotion; they're far superior to the prison-issue ones. Once when Terri took two extra and tucked them in her pocket, I said, "You just come for the tissues." She smiled on her way out the door.

So what happens when someone pours out her problems and you know you can't fix them? *You become a better listener.* You realize your presence—the loving regard of a person who knows her truth and doesn't flinch—has an inestimable value, perhaps even greater than the short-term fixes you might have liked to offer. You get to remind her that she is a precious child of God. She may not have ever heard that before, having lived much of her life being called "stupid" and "loser" and worse.

When I had access to my "bag of tricks," that's what I went for, way too quickly. It wasn't that I wouldn't take time to listen to the person's story. But I made the assumption that she had come to me for the resources, for the referral, for the next steps. My pastor friend Cindy tells of a time she reached for the phone and her visitor said, "Aren't you going to pray for me?" I couldn't see that I had something to offer, simply in my presence and my openness, beyond any tangible aid.[6]

I think now that—in those years before my church was in prison—it felt too hard to stay present as the person shared from a place of deep pain. I would use "fixing" as a way to distance myself. If I sit with you in the pain of the moment, I have to feel that pain, too—the pain of unfairness, disappointment, wrongdoing, dashed expectations, and more. I can wall myself off from all of that hurt, but along the way I wall myself off from *you*.

---

5. Learn more about Al-Anon at https://al-anon.org/.

6. I also admit that many people who come to a church for help are only looking for tangible aid, and they'll move on if they don't receive that, in short order. But even that observation doesn't let us church folk off the hook. Behind that pattern of behavior is surely a whole history of approaches and rebuffs, in which time and presence were poorly offered. Would it have made a difference to that person's story if, early on, she had been warmly welcomed, and embraced, and *heard*?

Foolish Church

It's no wonder that so many church mission projects entail helping at a distance. We spend a lot of time and energy collecting things like food, clothing, and money. We figure out who's going to drop it off on our behalf, and we're proud to report our results on Sunday morning. It doesn't occur to us that in all of that effort, we never interacted with the persons who would receive what we gave.

We go on mission trips to distant places where we intensely help for four days. (We're actually there for five, but usually we get the day or afternoon off on Wednesday for fun and souvenirs.[7]) Then we head home with stories of what we accomplished and perhaps a few memories of the people whose cares we sought to alleviate. But our focus has been the work, and what we have gotten built, or renovated, or cleaned up.

I speak from experience: I've been on more than a dozen mission trips, usually leading the team. I've found great joy and connection in the work and travels with the good folk who have journeyed with me. We have learned about the situation that led us to this place: storm damage, poverty, aging buildings, or our nation's treatment of Native American peoples. We have heard from representatives of the ministries that hosted us, and we've been moved by their tenacity and drive. But in all of these mission trips, I cannot remember more than a handful of face-to-face conversations with the people whose homes we repaired. Even when we met those people, I don't remember taking much time to hear their stories. Never have I remained in touch with them after the trip. We were there with a job to do. Finishing that project seemed much more important than actually *seeing* and coming to know the people who lived there, and what they need, and what resources they already have in place.[8]

I am saddened when parents use mission settings as object lessons for their children: "Do you see now how good you have it?" Or when we spend our energy criticizing the choices those recipients have made: "Did you notice that family we're helping has a cell phone and cable TV?" Even today when I'm asked to talk to young people, it sometimes seems like I'm supposed to warn them against prison-bound behavior—"scare them

7. For some mission sites, that time "off" is an important day when the local staff and volunteers can recharge.

8. I now question this whole enterprise. See the important critique in Corbett and Fikkert, *When Helping Hurts*, chapter 7; Lupton, *Toxic Charity*, 13–18.

20

straight," as in the 1978 documentary[9]—rather than share the good work we do among dear women.

Pretty soon our missions take on an ominous *us* and *them* message. *We* get set up as generous helpers for *them* ("those people"), who desperately need us. We get to be the heroes. We have expertise, time, and money that we graciously bestow on recipients we hope will appreciate what we've done. We feel proud of what we accomplished. But we don't learn very much when mission happens this way. It doesn't occur to us that "those people" might have wisdom and creativity that could enrich us, were we to know them. We rarely include them in the design and execution of our mission plan. Along the way, "those people" begin to internalize our message that they don't have anything to offer, which leaves them increasingly dependent and unlikely to volunteer the resources and wisdom they carry.[10]

Years ago, I was part of a team that would serve a meal once a month at a church basement in Des Moines. I had done this several times when I read something that Rev. Denny Coon, the pastor of that church, wrote to us earnest volunteers. "Get out from behind the line!" he said. I knew immediately, to my shame, what he meant.

I had been quite happy to take my place behind the line of tables that held plates and plastic ware next to warmers and platters full of steaming food. I stood there with a beneficent smile that I would bestow from a small but reassuring distance upon those hungry people as they arrived. Once in a while, if I hadn't managed to claim my place early enough next to the warmer that held, say, green beans that needed me to dish them out, I might have to come out from behind that line to carry a tray for a person with a cane or a toddler. And as the meal was ending, if I didn't get to the dishwashing area soon enough, I might have to walk out into that mass of tables and people to clear and wipe down tables. Coming out from behind the line was not where I wanted to be.

But now Pastor Denny was saying to me, "Get out from behind the line!" He urged us to take a seat at the tables, and actually converse with the people. As uncomfortable as that sounded to me, I could see the wisdom in his words. I steeled myself to do that the next time I visited. I watched for an opportunity, and I sat myself down at a table with four or five hungry people who had come that night, ready to talk with them.

9. Shapiro, *Scared Straight*.

10. Corbett and Fikkert, *When Helping Hurts*, 61–64; Lupton, *Toxic Charity*, 34, 37–49.

And I had no idea what to say. What did I have in common with these hungry people? (Do you notice that's all I could see of them?) I didn't even bring a plate, because this food was for them, not me; *I* wasn't a hungry person! I sat there feeling the weight of Pastor Denny's wise words, as conversation moved among the rest of the people at that table. In that moment, I was the one feeling famished, in a different way than they had been.

When guests join us for worship at the prison, they sometimes wonder what they can talk about. These groups know they'll be sitting with the residents who are joining in worship. "Don't just sit in a clump with your whole group," we'll tell them. "Sit in ones and twos, and it's always better if you sit next to one of the women, so you can talk." Sometimes these guests will come right out and ask what they can talk about. Almost everyone comes with the innate wisdom not to ask, "Whatcha in for?" But knowing what *not* to ask doesn't help people know where to start. "Ask about the food," I'll say. "Or what her room is like. Or does she have a job?" Once the conversation starts, it takes on a life of its own.

That happens, too, in the conversations I have one-on-one. Sometimes she comes with a very clear request. "I want you to pray for my parole," announced one woman whom I had never met, as she burst into my office. Some are less ready to say why they've come, so I've learned to begin with small talk. Where are you from? Have you been here long? Either way, I find the conversation soon goes deeper. I try to notice what brings tears to her eyes, and where she gets energized, whether with delight or rage. Once I see that spark, I know we're getting to what's important.

I used to have the opportunity for conversation with nearly every resident as she got ready to leave prison. Back then, she had to check out of various parts of the institution, so even women who had never once been inside the Sacred Place would come by and ask me to sign their papers. That interaction ended up being rich and meaningful.

"Are you excited?" I'd ask, as she handed me her paper, and she would of course express her delight that she was leaving in a few days. If time permitted I might ask where she was headed, and who was waiting for her there, and she would usually share that information with glee. I found, though, that if I could squeeze in just one more question—something like "How will it be, going there?"—almost to a person she would look at me with her guard finally down. "I'm scared to death." "I'm going right back where I got in trouble before." "I don't know how I'm going to manage it." I learned a lot from those encounters. There is pain and fear behind so many smiles. If we persist just a little, we may find out what she could barely admit, even to herself.

Upon uncovering that, the next step is not to devise strategies to solve that problem for her. Sure, there are systemic ills that might arise again and again, and there is a time and place to address those, as we'll discuss in chapter 3. But in that moment, with that human being, our first impulse must be to listen, and not to flinch. Our role is to hear, and care, and allow our common humanity with this person to become manifest in that room.[11] Usually I'll ask if I can pray with her, but first I want her to feel heard, and loved.

In their excellent book on neighboring, Jay Pathak and Dave Runyon tell of a conversation some pastors had with their city's mayor. He complained that people would see something wrong and then immediately call the city and say, "This is becoming a serious issue, and you should start a program to address it."[12] This mayor said he thought many of the issues facing that city could be addressed "if we could just figure out a way to become a community of great neighbors."[13] The pastors heard in these words a challenge of biblical proportions: Isn't one of Jesus' basic instructions— part of the Great Commandment (Matt 22:37–40)[14]—that we are to love our neighbors? Why are we so quick to spiritualize those words and think in terms of Samaritans and persons lying in a ditch, rather than the people who live right next to us?[15]

These authors offer three reasons why it's so hard for us to love our neighbor: isolation, fear, and misunderstanding.[16] All three of these rea-

11. I am grateful to Desmond Tutu and Mpho Tutu for their clarity and teaching about our common humanity, rooted in the concept of *Ubuntu*. "The word literally means 'humanity.' It is the philosophy and belief that a person is only a person through other people. . . . Our humanity is bound up in one another, and any tear in the fabric of connection between us must be repaired for us all to be made whole. This interconnectedness is the very root of who we are." Tutu and Tutu, *Book of Forgiving*, 8.

12. Pathak and Runyon, *Art of Neighboring*, 19. Some good resources on this subject can be found at Block and McKnight, "Abundant Community," and at Block et al., *An Other Kingdom*.

13. Pathak and Runyon, *Art of Neighboring*, 19.

14. We discuss this commandment below; see also Galatians 5:14.

15. Pathak and Runyon, *Art of Neighboring*, 35. The story of the Good Samaritan appears at Luke 10:25–37.

16. Pathak and Runyon, *Art of Neighboring*, 29–30.

sons are illustrated in a story from their book: A man called the city's code enforcement officials when his neighbor's house was visibly run down, with a garage door that was falling off of its hinges and two derelict cars on the lawn. The city ticketed the house, but shortly thereafter this man learned the rest of the story: The owner lived alone, and had quit her job to care for her mother who had cancer. "She's been by her mom's bedside twenty-four hours a day for the past few months," he learned.[17]

This story exemplifies those three reasons we aren't always generous with our neighbors: This man was *isolated* from this neighbor; he didn't know her. He was *fearful* of what kind of people would live like that. And he didn't know—he *misunderstood*—the circumstances that explained the mess. Knowing the rest of the story changed this neighbor's perceptions and led him to offer personal assistance to change that neighbor's circumstances.[18]

When I first went to the prison, those three circumstances—isolation, fear, and misunderstanding—were absolutely present for me. I wondered: How would I be compassionate to these women who had made choices I was sure I would never make? I've lived a rather comfortable and upright life. I wondered how I would love these people! This was troubling, because I believe *loving the people* describes my most basic work as a pastor. Looking back, those doubts illustrate the very reasons why neighboring is hard, as we just talked about. I didn't know anyone who had been in prison; I plainly was *isolated* from them. This population could be dangerous; there's reason for *fear!* I was sure their decisions were, by definition, indefensible. Could that be me, *misunderstanding* them?

The answer began to emerge nearly as soon as I started talking to the women I met at the prison. I began to hear their stories. I laughed with them, and found myself admiring their courage. I handed them a soft tissue to dry their tears and found I needed one myself. My question shifted from "How could she do what she did?" to "After all she's been through, how is she still standing?" Time and presence pushed me past the isolation, fear, and misunderstanding, and I began to become someone who could enter into real relationship with women I never would have had the heart to seek out.

17. Ibid, 30.
18. Ibid.

I have come to believe that those rules about what I cannot do to help women inside the prison are exactly what makes me most helpful there. The things that make *me* focus on presence, and listening, and relationship help *them*, too. They don't come to me expecting some kind of favor, or fix, or solution. They come knowing they'll be met with compassion, welcome, and, indeed, *love*.

One of my joys is getting to notice the things a person is doing right. When she's working on so many changes, it can be hard. "I say I'm gonna stop lying, Pastor Lee," she'll say, "but then I find myself doing it." For her, this is evidence that she'll never solve this problem. I get to see it differently. "Sure," I might respond, "but think of all the lies you told and it never bothered you. The first step toward not lying is noticing when you do." She'll look at me with a slow smile and say, "I never thought of it that way." I get to cheer her on with each halting step.

Relationship there, even within the bounds of prison, means caring deeply through the messes. It means that I could joke with Jodi who arrived back in prison describing the suicide pact with her boyfriend in which they both ingested pills and a few bottles of Miller Light. I looked her straight in the eye and I said, "I guess I'm glad it was Miller *Light*." She laughed with understanding, and I smiled at her precious face, relieved that the suicide attempt had failed. Relationship means that I could join Robin in a ritual to grieve the ending of her marriage, in which she unraveled some knitting as a way of mourning what was lost. Relationship means that Terri and I can say to each other with absolute sincerity, "I miss your face," as we do, across months and years when we are unable to see one another. Relationship means that Janice, working through a forgiveness study with me, could take seriously the assignment to make a list of all the things she needed forgiven.[19] When she came for our next meeting, she looked uncharacteristically nervous, and before she even reached my doorway, she cried, "I'm afraid you won't look at me the same way after I read this list." We sat together as she read it to me, in the safety of our mutual regard, and never after has she doubted that I could listen without giving up on her.

———

The alternative is untenable. Glennon Doyle Melton illustrates this in her book *Love Warrior*, in which she describes being sent to a priest when she is deep in despair over abortion, addiction, and estrangement even

19. See chapter one, note 9.

from her own self.[20] While waiting, she glimpses something true, warm, and welcoming in the sanctuary with red velvet carpet, a tray of flickering candles and a huge painting of Mary holding her baby Jesus.

> Mary is lit up bright and I am in soft, forgiving light. She is wearing a gown and her face is clear. I am wearing a tube top and my face is dirty, but she is not mad at me so I do not bother to cover myself. . . . She is what I needed. She is the hiding place I've been looking for.[21]

Melton's time with Mary is interrupted when the priest comes. "I can tell he's trying not to look surprised as he takes in my clothes, my face, my bare feet. He looks surprised anyway." He leads her to his cold office where she sits in a plastic chair with his large desk between them. His words, but not his demeanor, offer a route to forgiveness. "He dismisses me in a way meant to assert his disapproval," Melton says. She longed for the acceptance the painting had conveyed. "Mary didn't ask me to repent. She asked me to rest."[22]

I want to be Mary in this scenario.

Parker Palmer names the truth that when we dismiss one another, when we disapprove of them, we are in a sense *killing them*. He says,

> when you say something that doesn't conform to or support my world view, then I find some way of killing you off . . . Not with a gas chamber or a bullet, but with a phrase of dismissal or diminution, to render you irrelevant to my life. And I think that's a fair definition of what it means to kill somebody off.[23]

In that sense, we *kill* people when we can't make room for them, when we let them know (overtly or implicitly) that their story is too much for us, that they aren't one of us. I don't want us church folk to do that anymore. The work of a church must be, first and always, to offer our presence with *love*.

———

Is it too much to say that the *best* thing we do as a church is real relationship? We might see relationship as an incomplete ideal unless it supports our higher Christian purposes: getting people saved, making disciples,

20. Melton, *Love Warrior*, 51.

21. Ibid., 54–55.

22. Ibid., 55–58.

23. Palmer, *An Undivided Life*. A recent article illustrates this, using the language of "cancelling" a person, or "throwing them away." Campbell, "Trauma Makes Weapons."

transforming the world. But if we approach relationship only as means to those ends, we can become manipulative. If you've ever begun to connect with someone you thought would be your friend and then discovered they just wanted to evangelize you, you know what I mean.

Jesus had high expectations of his closest followers; he directed them in Matthew 28:19 to go and make disciples. But their preparation was grounded in relationship. "I have called you friends," Jesus said, among his final words to his disciples (John 15:15). He made it clear that our first and greatest commandment is love:

> "You shall love the Lord your God with all your heart, and with all your soul, and with all your mind." This is the greatest and first commandment. And a second is like it: "You shall love your neighbor as yourself." On these two commandments hang all the law and the prophets. (Matt 22:37–40)

When we're in real relationships, the rest is possible—salvation, discipleship, transformation—in a sustained and not mechanistic way. Everything we do as a church hangs on love.

The first and best thing we do as a church is enter into real relationships with real human beings.

How do we become churches—and church people!—that specialize in relationships?

We begin loving people beyond our own families. We receive a lot of messages that reinforce a family-centered view of life. I see memes regularly that announce "Family is everything." Princess Diana reportedly said, "Family is the most important thing in the world." A local grocery store, Fareway, sells new ingredients and recipes with this tag line: "Remember, the most important ingredient in any recipe is *family.*"

I wince at words like that. I wince because I know a lot of women who are cut off from their families. Sometimes that has to do with her behavior, or her crime, and understandable exhaustion and boundary-setting within her family. Sometimes painful family relationships come out of abuse and trauma she experienced from a young age, made worse because they originated among the family members who were supposed to protect her. Whatever causes this brokenness, the drum-beat of "family, *family*, FAMILY" accentuates the distance between her experience and the family she would have wanted. It's painful.

Not to mention that few of us have life experiences that match our culture's romanticized picture of "family." There's a tension there, right? Some of us might know "family" as great relationships and lots of hugs and laughs that we can't wait to share. But there's a reason movies and articles satirize how quickly many of us want to get through that family time at the holidays. Family is complicated.

There's a deeper reason, though, to wince at words that idealize, and even idolize, *family*. They narrow our thinking! Jesus calls us to love God *and neighbor* (Matt 22:37–40); that's a bigger vision than family alone. Messages that our families are the most important thing—as if they're the *only* thing!—let us off the hook. There's so much more to life, beyond our families. Our lives are enriched when we come to know and love people whose stories and experiences are very different from our own.

For me, that didn't happen by deciding I needed more relationships. It happened when I found myself where I didn't plan to go, and then found myself surprised to love the people I met there. Where might that happen, for you?

We do the things friends do. I heard a man in prison talk about what he hoped for from church people, upon his release. He said, "Invite me, like you would a friend!" He wasn't talking about church services; he meant community events. "You're going to the county fair? Ask if I want to go along. You're having a cookout at the local park? Ask me whether I'm free! Offer to give me a ride, if I need one, and just enjoy spending time with me!" Along the way, we might discover he makes a mean pot of chili, and pretty soon we'll be swapping recipes.

Our first thought about our friends is not how we might help them. We think about activities we might do together, and stories we want to tell them. Along the way, we might do favors for one another and, in many friendships, there will be times where one helps another through a particular challenge. But a good friendship doesn't look like all giving on one side, and all receiving on the other.

When I served a church outside the prison, I used to lament that people who first came there for a particular program—AA, our medical clinic, a free garage "sale"—didn't seem to get connected as members of the church. I would put flyers and table tents in those spaces, announcing our upcoming potluck, worship series, or the small group that was starting. Yet to my knowledge, not a single person who first entered our building as a beneficiary of one of these mission programs ever connected within the church as a member, in a genuine, personal relationship with others who attended there. The person who first comes for *help* is unlikely to ever see herself as a part of the community, on the same footing with everyone else there.

This brings me back to our churches' mission projects. One way to test our motives might be to think about those people that we're serving and ask this question: If some of them came and sat next to us in church, would we welcome them with open hearts? If we can't say yes to that, then we'd better look long and hard at what we're up to. We have to be about relationship first, and then helping. There may indeed be room to offer some help. But let it be born of relationship.

We see one another as grown-ups. Real relationship doesn't look like you, the expert, telling me, the brainless, what to do. It isn't you, the grown-up, advising me as if I were a child. Relationship involves mutuality, with give and take, where you and I feel like peers. It will take time. We'll both have to be vulnerable with one another.

Notice how this unfolds when Jesus meets the Samaritan woman at the well, in John 4. This story—for which our prison congregation is named—came alive for me when readers presented it theater style at the prison. A formidable African American woman, Tatiana, delivered the woman's words with more moxie than I had ever attributed to this unnamed woman, and I heard for the first time how Jesus met her many questions openly and respectfully. Jesus did not react to the Samaritan woman as a dreadful sinner whom he needed to fix.[24] He welcomed her questions and responded with one truth after another that freed her in turn to respond and share truth with others.

We don't always do this very well, especially when we meet people who seem needy or less confident. I worry about this when we match a woman leaving prison with a reentry team. These teams are four to seven people from a local church who have been recruited and trained to serve as a support group for her during the first year after she leaves prison. I sat with one such team, newly introduced to Ariana, who was going to leave prison soon. In the forty-five minutes they spent with her, members of the

24. See Lose, "Misogyny, Moralism and the Woman at the Well"; Reader, "Revisiting the Woman at the Well."

team asked Ariana a number of questions about her plans and expectations, responding to each of her answers with their own advice, which Ariana had not actually requested. When Ariana mentioned a fiancé, they all but told her to forget about him, without asking a single question about his circumstances or their relationship. While I'm certain her team meant to be helpful and caring, it seemed Ariana left that conversation with a sense of distance that was never fully healed.

Parker Palmer commends the practice of asking what he calls "honest and open questions."[25] He encourages groups to understand that they aren't there to fix, save, advise, or correct each other.[26] Instead, our questions should "invite a speaker to reach for deeper and truer speech."[27] Honest, open questions are not aimed at eliciting what we regard as the "right" answer; they are questions whose answers we cannot possibly know.[28] So, instead of "Why would you want to spend time with that deadbeat Steve?" an honest, open question might wonder "How does your relationship with Steve make you happier?" or "What does he bring to the relationship, or to your life?" When we are asked such questions, Palmer says, our "soul feels welcome to speak its truth . . . because they harbor no hidden agendas."[29] Persons both answering *and asking* the questions will be stronger when conversation is conducted in this spirit.

It won't always be easy, especially when the person we meet isn't making what we would consider good choices. We may desperately want to tell her what to do, to avoid the pit straight ahead. When she falls into it, it will be hard to stay the course with her, and we'll be tempted to blame and try to fix her all over again. We have to work to stay open to her, even through those times. It's what Sara Groves sings in "Like a Lake": "When everything in me is tightening, curling in around this ache, I will lay my heart wide open like the surface of a lake."[30]

25. Palmer, *Hidden Wholeness*, 130.

26. Ibid., 217.

27. Ibid., 130.

28. Ibid., 132.

29. Ibid.

30. Groves, "Like a Lake." © 2009 Sara Groves Music (admin. by Music Services) All Rights Reserved. ASCAP. Used by permission.

Jesus, looking at him, loved him (Mark 10:21a).

A man whom tradition identifies as the "rich young ruler" came to Jesus in a hurry, as Jesus was setting out on a journey (Mark 10:17). The man didn't introduce himself; he simply ran up, knelt down and blurted out, "Good Teacher, what must I do to inherit eternal life?" (10:17). One might say he was looking for a *program*. He wanted an answer, and quickly.

Jesus responded by reciting some of the commandments (10:18–19). But the man has heard all this before; "Teacher, I have kept all these since my youth," he interjects (10:20), and looks expectantly for some more personal instruction from Jesus.

In a moment, Jesus will tell the man what to do. It's a hard edict: he is to sell his possessions, give the money away, and then come and follow Jesus (10:21). Mark tells us that the man could not accept these words; he went away grieving (10:22). This wasn't the program he wanted.

But before all that happens, before Jesus gives his prescription, he offers something more important. Mark pauses to tell us that "Jesus, looking at him, *loved* him" (10:21a). What an important detail. Even in this brief meeting, Jesus looked past this man's haste and bravado, past his fine clothing and his self-sufficiency, past his insistent questioning. Past all of that, and surely knowing the man would be unable to accept his instruction, Jesus *loved*.

Whatever programs we offer, and before anything we dispense, we must first *love*.

Sometimes that hurt, the pit where our new friend just fell, is connected to injustices that affect not just her, but many others. As we come into relationship with different people, we'll become aware of legal and cultural challenges that we hadn't noticed before. We may be moved to take action, or advocate for changes to help not just our friend, but others who are similarly bound. We'll talk about that in chapter 3.

Questions:

a. Tell about someone you've met in church who has made a positive difference in your life. Have you met people you wouldn't have known otherwise? How has this experience changed you for the better?

b. Has your church dealt with questions of how to love someone who was challenging? How did that play out? What values were expressed along the way?

c. Do you feel it is sometimes easier to help people through some program than to enter into a personal relationship with them? What hard things are you seeking to avoid? What are your worries about opening yourself up to an actual relationship?

d. How is a church strengthened when it is built on relationship with real human beings rather than programs to serve people's perceived needs?

e. Whom is God calling you to come to know and love as a person, rather than to focus on meeting his or her needs?

3

The Church Believes and Protects

How could anyone ever tell you
you were anything less than beautiful?
How could anyone ever tell you
you were less than whole?
How could anyone fail to notice
that your loving is a miracle?
How deeply you're connected to my soul.

—LIBBY RODERICK[1]

The day the parole board met to decide Kristina Fetters's fate, we all held our breath. Kristina was a "lifer," a woman who had been, at the age of fifteen, sentenced to prison without the possibility of parole for the murder of her great-aunt.[2] After she was diagnosed with terminal breast cancer and a plan was made to send her to hospice, I wasn't sure whether there would be joy or outrage among her fellow prison residents if the parole board agreed. When the "yes" came late that December morning, there

1. Lyrics reprinted from "How Could Anyone," by Libby Roderick.
2. Rodgers, "Woman sentenced to life as juvenile paroled to hospice." A summary of the court decisions that declared mandatory life sentences for juvenile offenders unconstitutional, and paved the way for Kristina Fetters's release, can be found at Rovner, "Juvenile Life without Parole."

were cheers, tears of relief, and words like "Praise the Lord!" I thought that day: *this is what mercy sounds like.*

An earlier December, I sat in the audience for my first WinterFest—a long-standing annual Christmas-themed "talent" show inside the prison that would attract hundreds of women as performers and audience members, until staffing and space constraints brought its end. I didn't know what to expect when Marie stood up to sing a solo, "The Twelve Days of Christmas." Marie was a gentle soul, kind and trusting, and unmistakably a member of the special needs population at the prison. She sang the first few verses of the song without incident but soon began to falter. What happens on the seventh day of Christmas, and the eighth? Marie sang without notes in her hand, and soon became visibly confused. I looked around wondering when the catcalls would start, and demands for her to come down off the stage. But that's not what happened. Instead there were words of encouragement, women calling out the missing words—"It's ten lords a-leaping, Marie!"—and "You're doin' great, Marie!" Soon the whole room was singing along. And Marie glowed at the center of it all, full of joy in that moment.

Prison isn't always like that; there's backbiting and people are victimized every day. But I've been surprised how often I witness support and encouragement. Women go out of their way with kindness and generosity for others who were strangers, not so long ago. Two women in solitary confinement find ways to communicate, talking and praying through the air vent or under their doors. Residents share their knowledge about which employers will hire someone after prison. Women in the visiting room come to care about one another's family members in the shreds of contact with each other that are allowed there. There is joy when a friend gets parole, even among those whose sentences will hold them inside for years. You walk across the yard and, almost as often as you hear women swearing (which is really often!), you'll hear one friend calling to another, "I love you."

Upon leaving prison, many of our women will find they are living in a much less supportive world. Deb, who finished a four-year prison term ten years ago, says, "Serving my sentence was the easy part. The real punishment was reentry." Reentry is hard because, out in society, ex-offenders don't typically find forgiving and generous communities. Their crimes continue to limit them and their opportunities. They are excluded from public housing, student loans, and in some states, including Iowa, the right to vote.[3] Many job applications get tossed out when employers see an "X" in the box that signifies an applicant's criminal history.[4] Those listed on a sex offender registry face even greater restrictions, including broad limits on where they can live, not to mention how they are regarded by the public.[5]

We say in prison that a person shouldn't have to be defined by the worst fifteen minutes of her life.[6] We don't mean that to be true only while she's in prison, but it often feels like people outside do. Our very language— ex-offender, felon, crook, delinquent—tends to define these friends according to their worst, hardest moments.

It's no wonder the disability community reminds us to use people-first language: not "she's bipolar," but "she has bipolar disorder"; not "those Down kids," but "those kids with Down syndrome."[7] The principle is that we should put the person first, before the condition or situation that affects her. I try to avoid the institutional language of "offender,"[8] but instead refer to "people who have been incarcerated," or "women" or "residents" for short. My friend Harold Dean Trulear and his co-authors helpfully propose the term "returning citizens" for those who are leaving prison.[9] I like the way that term emphasizes what we have in common as citizens, and that these folks are coming back to us—"returning," even if they're starting over in a new locale.

I've started over a few times in my life, and I've never had to worry much about how I would be received. Sure, part of me is still that girl I was in junior high, that geeky non-athletic goody-two-shoes who will never be the life of the party. But as a grown-up I know myself also to be smart, capable, resourceful, creative, and determined. With all of that, and with

---

3. Malcolm, "Collateral Consequences"; Legal Action Center, *After Prison.*

4. Some jurisdictions have adopted "ban the box" rules to minimize this barrier. Avery, "Ban the Box."

5. Human Rights Watch, "More Harm Than Good."

6. I am indebted to Dr. Harold Dean Trulear and Rev. Douglas Walker for articulating this truth, which they in turn attribute to Rev. Dr. Lonnie McLeod and to a young man named Keeneth who was on death row in Nashville. See also Stevenson, *Just Mercy,* 17–18; Goode et al., *Ministry with Prisoners,* 8.

7. For example, see this poster from the Centers for Disease Control: https://www.cdc.gov/ncbddd/disabilityandhealth/pdf/disabilityposter_photos.pdf.

8. The Iowa Department of Corrections is itself in transition over this language, often using the word "clients" in place of what had been the standard "offenders."

9. Goode et al., *Ministry with Prisoners,* 8.

awareness of my inherent privilege as a white, heterosexual, cisgender woman without physical or mental disabilities, I have experienced a world relatively open to who I am and what I want to accomplish. I carry that unearned privilege into every social interaction. This means I can walk into most rooms with least a decent chance of being treated with respect, of making a positive connection with a new acquaintance if there is one to be had there, and of moving toward the purpose that brought me there. What I say will generally be taken at face value, and most people will give me the benefit of the doubt.

I don't have a scarlet letter emblazoned on my cloak. When people see me, they probably aren't thinking about the worst thing I ever did. Searching my name online won't take you to a sex offender registry. I generally don't have to worry that the woman over there is whispering to her friend that I'm that one who [fill in the blank], and I don't have to bear up under their scrutiny before they look away in disgust.

Most of what I just described I did not earn. Some is an accident of birth,[10] some a result of being raised among loving people who were, in turn, raised in homes that didn't know violence, mental illness, addiction, crime, or neglect. The withering history of discrimination against persons of color in this country did not touch my Dutch, Anglo-Saxon, and Scotch-Irish ancestors, except as beneficiaries of it. No one in my family has, to my knowledge, been stopped and questioned by police on suspicion of anything more serious than a speeding ticket.

Growing up, I couldn't see any of this. School taught me that I was special because of my good grades and award-winning projects. It also taught me who the "losers" were, from very early in elementary school. They were the ones with ragged and dirty clothes, unfinished homework, occasional detentions and frequent absences, and reading skills that vexed me every time we would read out loud as a class. I felt tortured by what I saw as their stupidity. It never occurred to me to wonder what pain they were experiencing.

I now look back at those childhood reactions through a whole different lens. I did not, as a child, have the vocabulary or life experience to wonder what life was like for those classmates I so readily counted as losers.

10. Warren Buffet calls this "winning the ovarian lottery." See Weisenthal, "What Warren Buffet Says." Robert Putnam lays out the lifelong consequences of choosing the wrong parents. Putnam, *Our Kids*. Cf. Tutu and Tutu, *Book of Forgiving*, 72–73 (arguing that the most important determinant for children's emotional health and resilience is knowing their families' stories, "the good, the bad, and the ugly").

I assumed their lives and homes were just like mine. Looking back, though, with what I know now, I wonder what role addiction, abuse, mental illness, poverty, and crime may have played in some of those families. My classmates were no more responsible for factors like these than I was for the encouraging, safe family that surrounded me.

In prison you come up against the extremity of human experience in ways that challenge every assumption about what "home" looks like. A person who commits a heinous act has probably lived through unspeakable circumstances. I think of one woman serving a long sentence whose young life was marked by abuse by two different stepfathers, and instability that included fifteen moves in three years, with no consistent schooling.[11]

When this woman sought commutation of a decades-long sentence in 2011, the parole board voted no, citing her "insufficient remorse" and their surprise that she had not sought other ways to deal with the abuse. The parole board chair said, "You lived right across the street from the sheriff. There were plenty of people you could have gone to for help."[12] That may seem evident to that chair of the parole board. But it's hard to see anything in this woman's story that would have made her think the sheriff would have acted to protect her. And it's not too much to ask: Would he? Domestic violence victims have not always been well served by law enforcement and other persons in authority.[13] The #MeToo movement has brought this truth more starkly into public conversation.

Those of us who come from places of safety and protection can find it hard to fathom the lives and choices of people around us. We don't understand why women don't leave the men who abuse them. We would never allow ourselves to be forced into delivering drugs or into prostitution, so we assume someone who does these things chose those actions willingly. But it's a mistake to judge someone else's life from the relative safety we may have known. In his book *Between the World and Me*, Ta-Nahesi Coates offers a window into life very different than I have known. Growing up on the streets of Baltimore, Coates knew from a very young age that he was "naked before the elements of the world," which for him included ever-present

11. Gribben, "Abuser, Lover, Stepfather."

12. Quoted in Ashkenazi, *The Grey Area*.

13. One first-person report of these challenges can be found at Simon, "Worked in the Domestic Violence Unit."

"guns, fists, knives, crack, rape, and disease."[14] He describes chillingly how death rose "up from the nothing of a boyish afternoon" one day when a boy next to him pulled out a gun.[15] As a sixth-grader at the time, this brought Coates face to face with the ghastly reality that his black body could "be erased," in an instant.[16]

Coates knew the truth that many of our residents have learned: Safety is a myth, and those who are supposed to protect us may not.[17] I hear about a lot of cries for help that were not heeded. Miranda was raped. Whitney was molested by her brother. When these women—as girls—told their mothers, Mom didn't believe them. Angela was sexually assaulted by several different men in her life—her grandfather, her uncle, a neighbor around the corner from where she lived. Her grandmother knew what had happened, but did nothing. Angela grew up thinking this was just the way things are; this was how people treat each other. In her world, she was right.

I have come to believe that the easiest thing in the world is to *disbelieve her.* We do it when women say they've been raped and when girls say they've been abused.[18] Our first question often is not, "How could he do that to you?" Instead, it's "What did you do to bring it on yourself?" We scrutinize what she was wearing, how she behaved, whether she was drinking, whether she ever encouraged his attentions, and what exactly was her history with other partners. Sexual assault is said to be terribly underreported—not least because of the negative attention such a report is sure to bring to the victim.[19]

Or, as some of our sisters' stories demonstrate, we might not ask any questions at all. We might just say, aloud or by our silence, that we don't believe her.

14. Coates, *Between the World and Me*, 17.

15. Ibid., 19–20.

16. Ibid., 19.

17. Coates makes a deeper point about these dangers: they are part of an intentional system that made his black body "breakable," in which the "nakedness" he felt "is not an error, not pathology. The nakedness is the correct and intended result of policy. . . . A society that protects some people through a safety net of schools, government-backed home loans, and ancestral wealth but can only protect you [i.e., if you are black] through the club of criminal justice has either failed at enforcing its good intentions or has succeeded at something much darker." Ibid., 17–18.

18. We do this same thing with boys who claim sexual assault.

19. RAINN, "Criminal Justice System: Statistics;" Engel, "Why Don't Victims."

It's so much simpler if we don't believe her. That person she's accusing might be my husband; our family depends on his income. Or it might be my son, whom I love. To follow up on her allegation would mean throwing any number of relationships and family dynamics into disarray. I'd have to *do* something—maybe a lot of things—that I don't want to do.

The easiest thing in the world is to disbelieve her.

I am particularly troubled when it's the church that's doing the disbelieving.

We've already talked about being the church that allows people to share their scars. When they do, and they tell their stories, will we believe them?

I had known Lori a long time before she told me her story of sexual violence, by her father. She wanted to confide in her pastor but found his wife at home instead. Lori told her what had happened, and the pastor's wife said they would be in touch soon. A few days later they followed up with Lori, sitting down with her and saying, "We've prayed about it, and God told us it didn't happen." When Lori protested, they went on, "If you keep lying about it, you're going to hell."[20]

I can't think of a single instance in which Jesus denied someone help because he didn't believe the story he or she told. A lot of people came to Jesus asking for help, sometimes for a family member or servant that was far off. Jesus heard their pleas and responded, again and again.

I didn't know how to take Paige's story of the infant son she had birthed and lost sixteen years before I met her. Her son was, Paige said, the fruit of molestation and incest by her grandfather who raised her. When Paige became pregnant, her grandparents kept her home from school. "We'll home-school her," she says they told the school. "She's not well." When her son was born—at home, without medical attention—Paige named and loved him. She remembers gazing into his eyes, "in synch," totally, in those first days. Then on her son's fifth day of life, she watched her grandfather suffocate him with a pillow and throw away his lifeless body in a shiny black garbage bag.

20. In a contrast that is no less disturbing, Suzanne's pastor didn't dispute the abuse she described to him, perpetrated by her husband. The pastor simply told her she should be less disagreeable and, after all, her husband had charge of the household.

Paige's grandparents are long dead. There is nothing to be done, upon hearing this story that Paige tells, except to decide whether to take it at face value, and respond to it, or to doubt that it ever happened.

I'll admit, I find myself wondering whether it did happen. I think I don't want to believe that this kind of thing happens, in Iowa, in my lifetime. If I disbelieve Paige, I don't have to think very hard about how harsh the world is. I don't have to wonder what else that family did to one another, or what failures of community and church and culture contributed to the atrocities she experienced.

I am thankful that it's not my job to ferret out the truth of Paige's story. I wouldn't know where to start. But I have a different job. You know what it is? It's to *believe her*. My work is to love Paige, and her truth, as she tells it. As one expression of that love, I worked with her and others to hold a memorial service for her son, dead these sixteen years, and for all that might have been, had he lived. We sang, and we prayed, and we offered again those timeless funeral prayers that remind us that "in our living and dying, [God] may be our peace."[21] It was a lovely, important time, and afterward Paige looked at me with tears in her eyes. "Thank you, Pastor Lee," she said. "I needed this. I've needed this for sixteen years."[22]

I have come to believe that inside the prison, as outside, we tell our truth in ways that may not be the full, unvarnished truth. Who among us has not experienced this? We come home from work and complain to a loved one—I'll call him Xavier—about how our boss spoke to us. We tell that story in a way intended to gain Xavier's support and encouragement. But our telling is likely not absolutely, historically true to what happened. We might leave out the detail where we accused our boss of playing favorites with that co-worker, or her reminder that she had warned us about our misbehavior once before. We probably speak our own words with a gentler tone, and hers more harshly, than they actually happened. In this scenario, Xavier's role is to believe us and be on our side—and if we tell our story well, it might startle us when he offers to take that boss of ours down

---

21. United Methodist Publishing House, *United Methodist Book of Worship*, 162.

22. I am mindful that there may be necessary limits on *believing her*. There are law enforcement and cultural questions that go beyond the immediacy of what I am advocating. See Weiss, "The Limits of 'Believe All Women.'" My pastoral response, though, and that of the church in which she finds herself, is to walk with her in her truth, as she tells it and understands it—now and perhaps as it unfolds over time.

a notch or two! We may realize then that it wasn't quite as bad as we made it sound.

This is how truth emerges. We tell what we can. We tell what we are able to face, for now, or what we think you our listener is ready to bear, about what happened. Maybe we are absolutely clear that we shaded the facts a bit in our favor. Maybe we don't even realize we're doing it. But for that moment, at least, that's our story.[23] We may tell it again later when we can face more of the truth, and our telling may shift—like it did for Tamara whom we met in chapter 1, who was finally able to admit her crime.

And the role of the church in this scenario is to be, well, *Xavier*. To be the one who hears the amount of truth that we can say today, and responds by believing us and encouraging us. Or at least *starts* with belief and encouragement, so that we know it was safe to share. The church must start with care and concern, rather than walls of doubt that try to talk us out of what we dared to put into words. There may be room later for truth-finding and re-examination. And very likely there *is* more to the story than we can tell right then. But especially in that first moment, to express care and support and a willingness to help? That's what The Church does for a hurting and broken world.

There are of course limits on what we can do for people who have set out to do harm. We'll talk about those situations in the next couple of chapters. The question here is: What is the church's role when something isn't right? When someone is in danger? Do we wave and drive on past, going about our own business? That's what happened when a neighbor saw a teenage Mariah out in the neighborhood park where she had fled without a coat or shoes on a late fall evening, afraid of her drunk, abusive father. Mariah was huddled there, feeling desperate and alone as it grew dark. When the neighbor went by, Mariah saw that she had recognized her. But even with the incongruity of Mariah's presence out there at that hour, inadequately dressed, the neighbor simply drove on. Is that what we can expect of the church? Or does the church have a role to play in responding to human need?

---

23. It is also possible that we are knowingly, deliberately lying. Even if that is the case, the response described here is the only response that can reasonably be brought to the situation, until further investigation or circumstances expose that lie. We meet people where they are, even in that dark and difficult place.

How much more would it have cost for that neighbor to stop, roll down the window, and ask, "Mariah, honey, what are you doing out here? Are you OK?"

I wonder how often we have been that neighbor, doing an instantaneous calculus: *What if* something is going on in her home, with her parents who are my friends, on this block where everyone is respectable? *What if* I found out something is wrong in her home; what would I do then?

I remember sitting at a scouting gathering, years ago, in the row behind a family I knew a little bit from church—dad, mom, a young son, and an older daughter. As people were gathering, that boy got into a tiny bit of mischief and made a small commotion. I watched as he spun his head, anxious, in the direction of his father, and his mom and sister immediately reacted, physically moving to place themselves between him and his dad, smoothing over what had just happened. In a moment, they saw that the dad hadn't budged from his seat, they all relaxed, and the moment passed.

It has never really passed, though, for me. I have wondered ever since: What was going on in that home? What would prompt the hyper-vigilance I observed, where every ounce of energy was instinctually engaged, to avert . . . *what*? I've thought of myself in this scene as *that neighbor*, seeing something that was not right and choosing not to say or do anything. I have justified my (non)response with the rationalization that I didn't see enough to be sure of anything. But I'm afraid I did. I missed an opportunity to extend care to that boy, and to that family. To this day, I'm not sure how I would have done it. But might there have been room for me to do *something*? Could I have reached out to this family, or at least initiated some kind of conversation with the mom? Could I have tried to walk with them in a different way, in light of what I saw?

For too long, churches have responded to victims of domestic violence with a mostly unhelpful shrug. Even when a church or pastor does not actively disbelieve or shame the person who is being abused, we often aren't sure what to do with her. So she is met with silence and minimal support. If the abuser is also active in the church, no one wants to disrupt the many relationships involved. Is this family a so-called "giving unit"? What are the implications for the church budget, if this issue blows up? Shame on us, if we let these questions become an excuse to do nothing. Our churches can and must be places where we listen to and believe the victim, where we help her identify and respond to dangers to herself and others, and where we help her connect with counseling and other helping services.[24] Nor can our care be limited to the victim. The perpetrator and victim may not both be able to remain in their current church, but the perpetrator must not be seen as having forfeited either the love of God or the care of the faith community by the actions that have come to light.[25]

When we, The Church, begin to face the tough truths of people's lives, domestic violence is just one of many issues we'll see. We'll have to respond to sexual violence such as rape and assault, and to suicide, whether threatened, attempted, or completed. We'll connect with persons who are the victims of a crime. There are law enforcement responsibilities, to be sure, but the church must be prepared to stand with persons who are being battered by the world. I once heard Sister Helen Prejean talk about families that have lost a loved one to murder. In an admittedly un-scientific survey of maybe twenty such families, she said, *every one of them* reported that they had felt abandoned by their church in the midst of their tragedy. This should not be! Even allowing that some families are going to pull away in such a time and not respond to sincere overtures from the church, the consistency of that happening for so many families should make us wonder how we can care *better*.

We can't fix everything. It's even more complicated when a church or its people are the source of the injury. We'll talk about this in the coming chapters. But in the midst of hurt and brokenness, the church must be a community that will be on the side of the hurting, that will turn aside to notice what doesn't look right, and that will help people to know they're not alone in facing the terrors this world can dish out.

We get to trust that the church is on our side.

So how do we become churches that believe and protect?

---

24. These suggestions are borrowed from United States Conference of Catholic Bishops, "When I Call for Help." See also Woodiwiss, *'I Believe You.'*

25. We cannot properly care for the victims of violence unless they are separated from their abuser. In such an instance, though, we have a responsibility not to simply put up walls against that person, but to express our willingness to connect the perpetrator with another local church where he or she can be welcomed and perhaps restored to relationship within the body of Christ. We may need to *be* that other church in our turn.

We notice. Whether it's Mariah in the park at twilight, or that family overreacting in a brightly lit gathering space, the first step is to notice what is going on around us. What doesn't look right? Why did that person respond that way? Is there more to the story than they just told us?

I suspect there are clues right in front of us, day by day, that we miss because we don't *want* to see. Seeing might require something of us, or sadden us. We might have to rethink what we know about someone, or it might challenge our assumptions about humanity in general. Sometimes we'd rather *not* notice.

What if we gave ourselves permission to work on *noticing* for a while without any pressure to take action? Maybe then we'd be willing to look with more curious eyes, more sustained attention, and more keen intuition. What might be going on with our neighbor, or that house down the block with all the stuff in their yard? Did that person just start to tell us something important, before we changed the subject or walked away? Could that friend's disappointing behavior come out of challenges they haven't shared?

We could take this too far, of course, and see hazard in every interaction. I'm not suggesting that we meet the world with paranoia! But I wonder: What would we notice if we were paying attention?

Our prison has offered a twice-yearly program called "The Domino Effect," aimed at school administrators, counselors, and teachers, in which some of our women tell their stories of what it was like for them in school.[26] Did they try to gain help along the way? How? Would it have made a difference if someone in their school had noticed the clues she was trying to drop? Miley has told how her grades went from straight "A's to nearly failing when she started getting abused. She dropped out of numerous extracurricular activities where she had excelled. But no one asked what was going on. Bethany tells that one day, in the midst of an intolerable situation at home, she intentionally put marijuana in her backpack, hoping that someone at school would find it, and follow up with questions and action. They did find it, she says. But the questions never came. She was punished with detention, and nothing changed. No one took the time to notice the desperation that led her to take that action.

We won't catch every situation. We won't know enough, or the family will hold their truth so closely that they wouldn't respond to our overtures

26. You can learn more about this program at https://thedominoeffectprogram.weebly.com/. It now includes both the women's prison and the men's maximum-security prison at Fort Madison, Iowa.

anyway. But noticing is the first step. We can't believe and stand up for people when we don't even hear them crying for help.

We care. A woman stopped me one morning in a church outside of prison and told me about her niece who is in jail in another state, dealing with drug addiction and complicated mental health issues. The girl's mother isn't helping; she doesn't accept that her daughter has a mental illness. The woman before me, the girl's aunt, had been in touch by phone and letter, and had put some money on the niece's account so that she could be in contact with her family. But she did not know what to do next.

I said, "You're doing an important thing by *caring* for her." It was clear that this seemed inadequate to her. "It's not so easy to care when you can't fix things for her," I said. "Good for you; you're helping her know she's not alone."

A critical step with any life challenge is to care for the person facing it. Mental illness, the criminal justice system, domestic violence, addiction, human trafficking: these are knotty, systemically complicated issues that defy resolution. We'll talk in a minute about how we can address these issues through advocacy and more. Before we get there, though, there's a need to care for our fellow human beings who are making their way through them.

Sometimes that care is going to hurt. It hurt—twice!—when Haley walked away from the halfway houses—two different ones!—that had been glad to receive her. I had come to care for Haley during her months in prison; I had worked to connect the dots between her prostitution charge and the human trafficking that lies behind it. I spent hours with Haley helping her see God at work in her life and the hope—the truth!—that she could live a good and holy life surrounded by people who loved her. Her walking away from that possibility hurts because I have to wonder what more I could have done. And it hurts because I'm disappointed in her. I don't *blame* her; life taught her at a very young age that she isn't worthy of seeking and receiving the help that is out there. I know enough about the hell she has lived through to imagine where she is now. In our last conversation, she said, "Either there's a halfway house for me or I'll end up in the grave."

I'm told it takes human trafficking victims, on average, seven or eight times of leaving that life before they are really free of it.[27] Domestic violence

27. Dickman, "Leaving Is Never Easy."

ministries cite similar statistics.[28] I pray for these survivors that they live long enough to get to that seventh or eighth time.

If we're going to care about these people, it's going to hurt. No question about it. If we've had good experiences of healthy relationships and human thriving, we'll find it hard when others cannot immediately incorporate those possibilities. But the price of protecting our own hearts is the abandonment of fellow human beings who desperately need to know that they're not alone. I'm not willing to pay—or to let them pay—that price. Let's *care*.

We act. This is perhaps the easiest and the hardest part of this chapter. We've noticed and we've cared; now please let us take *action!* There is a place for action. But it may not look like we expected.

Action is mostly not *fixing* things. How many times have I said there are a lot of things we cannot fix? We want to protect someone from an abuser, or find a safe place where her mental illness can be addressed, or rail against a legal system that puts her in prison for what seems like an unconscionably long period of time. We may not be able to accomplish these things.

Where we can assist someone to navigate a particular medical, legal, or other system, great. That's a meaningful action we can take. But I'm not advocating here that we take upon ourselves the whole responsibility for their defense, or their care, or their survival. So many challenging and often broken systems are involved in every one of these stories. Trying to rescue other people puts us in an unhealthy place. We'll talk more about this in chapter 4.

Still, it matters when people know they aren't alone. There may be room to accompany them, encourage them, and remind them of their best selves and their intrinsic worth. We may be able to support them in problem solving that will yield the best possible outcome. Sometimes this will have a great result. But sometimes they'll still go to prison, still end up on the street, still lose themselves in their addiction, still go back to the life they've known for years. We can still care, and still pray, even if we can't solve what has happened.

28. National Domestic Violence Hotline, "50 Obstacles to Leaving" (and subsequent articles in that series); Buel, "Fifty Obstacles to Leaving."

> *So he set off and went to his father. But while he was still far off,*
> *his father saw him and was filled with compassion; he ran and*
> *put his arms around him and kissed him.* (Luke 15:20)

Take a moment to read again the story of the Prodigal Son in
Luke 15:11–32. It's a rich and important story of greed and misbehavior by a son who wants to figure things out on his own. It includes a
reckoning, and a return, when that son figures out his best option is to
go back to his father, hat in hand. As the son trudges in his direction,
his father is already watching for his return. The son is still a long way
off when Dad sees him and is "filled with compassion"(15:20). He runs
to his son, embracing him with kisses and, soon, a robe, a ring, and a
feast (15:20–24).

We are meant to see God in this father. Here we glimpse how far
God will go to be on our side, no matter what we've done, even if our
repentance is self-serving and incomplete. Jesus makes it clear: We are
not alone—not against the world, nor against our older, respectable
sibling (15:25–32). "Come and join me in celebrating," the father says.
"The one we thought was dead is alive!"

And there's still room for action, even if that person is lost to us.
Maybe we are called to become advocates for people like her, who will otherwise be caught by an unjust law or system. Maybe there's a role for us
in a peacemaking circle[29] or mediation program aimed at helping persons
facing similar risks, or to educate others about the racial disparities we considered in the introduction. We act on behalf of—and alongside—persons
who have not always been able to speak for themselves, or whose voices
have not been heard. We cooperate with God's work in the world to eliminate injustice and to create a more supportive community. We persist in
that work long after the particular person whose needs inspired our energy
has moved beyond our reach.

Questions:

a. Remember and describe a time when your church stood up for a person by advocating for him or her, or offering tangible assistance. What

29. See Pranis, *Circle Processes.*

47

made that possible? What underlying values motivated that response? Did it make a difference for the person involved?

b. Are there times when your church has faced heavy questions of whether or not to believe someone? In what ways has this made it harder to believe one another?

c. What does it feel like when you tell your truth and you are not believed? How does that experience color your response to others when they tell their stories?

d. How is a church strengthened when it surrounds a person with support and protection? What fears keep us from doing so? Is there a middle ground?

e. Name one or two specific steps you can take to stand with persons who need you to be on their side. Are there things you need to learn about? (Domestic violence or addiction, for instance. Or how to advocate effectively for changes in legislation.)[30] How might you prepare your heart for this work?

---

30. For a helpful resource in this connection, see Mefford, *The Fig Tree Revolution.*

4

The Church Builds Boundaries, Not Walls

Your love, O God, is broad like beach and meadow,
wide as the wind, and our eternal home.

—FRED KAAN[1]

No one ever begged me for baptism until I found myself at Women at the Well. Inside the prison, it happens pretty often. She has met God through Jesus Christ at some point on her way to prison, or after she arrived, and now her faith has become a lifeline.

Jasmine was one of those who begged. She had missed the long-planned baptism service we held on Thanksgiving. She came to me the week after Christmas, with her ever-so-fervent request: Please would I baptize her before she left prison in a couple of weeks? Like so many women with whom I've had this conversation, she wanted to take that step, bear that marker, *before* she walked through those gates and out into the world.

"Yes," I told her. "We'll make it work." And we did, that very week. It required some rearranging. I needed to fit in some conversations with Jasmine, and it changed what would happen in worship that Thursday

---

1. Fred Kaan, translating Anders Frostenson, "Your Love, O God," reprinted in United Methodist Publishing House, *UM Hymnal*, 120. © 1974 Hope Publishing Company, Carol Stream, IL 60188. All rights reserved. Used by permission.

night. But we began the new year with baptism, Jasmine's hair glistening with water.

My go-to response to questions like these is always *yes*. There's nearly always a way to say *yes*, even if it means rearranging what I meant to do, or settling some details to make it possible. *Yes* is a response to which I've always been oriented, having heard it so regularly all my life. It's the response I most want people to hear from our churches, on the questions where it matters. "Yes, of course." "Sure." "We can do that."

My commitment to *yes* has been heightened by living in an environment of *no* for the past several years. I've gotten a lot of *no*'s at the prison. *No* to various programs we wanted to offer. *No* to some props—a couple of hats!—that we had requested for the first grown-up Vacation Bible School we offered our residents. *No*, for a time, to the use of real bread for communion. I actually wept over that one, wondering how those dry wafers could be the body of Christ.

No is, of course, the reality of prison for those who live there. Not just the big *NO* to your hope of avoiding time behind bars, but the thousands of smaller *no*'s that follow: the *no* of your counselor who doesn't have time to see you; the *no* of the parole board that says you haven't served enough time; the *no* of a job lost for a reason not fully understood; the *no* of a refused phone call, or a disconnected number without a new one communicated; the *no* of the halfway house, or your mom and dad, that you had thought might offer a haven for you upon your release.

Prison has taught me the shrewdness of *no*. It's the easiest possible response. *No* takes no effort and attention. It doesn't require any creativity. Especially when you don't feel compelled to offer reasons and explanations, it ends the conversation. *No*. End of story. Move along. Nothing to see here.

That kind of *no*, however, enlightens no one, strengthens no relationship, builds no leadership, and encourages no growth. It's a wall, a barrier we find ourselves stretching to see over, or looking for gaps to peer through, trying to figure out what it would take to get to the other side.

I find myself in a world where the church increasingly looks like *no*. Sadly, we are becoming known more for the things we are against than the things we are for. News stories highlight how walled-off we church people are. Christian believers and clergy get portrayed on TV and in the movies as judgmental and rigid, more interested in keeping people out than making space for a diversity of persons, opinions, and behaviors. Even among those of us who are quick to point out that not all Christians agree—"Please don't paint me with that inflexible brush!"—the perception of the church as hostile encumbers everything we try to do as church.[2]

It almost surprises me when a stranger walks into our churches. When she does, what will she find? Things that feel familiar and manageable to a church person could be an obstacle—a wall—for someone who is unfamiliar with our buildings and customs. Have you looked at yours recently? What feels like beauty and stability to me may feel forbidding to someone who's struggling to put one foot in front of the other. "Who would dare to walk in there?" she might wonder. "That place isn't *for* people like me."

If she does come, will people welcome her? Years ago, a couple walked in to my church, both of them with large, visible tattoos. I greeted them with enthusiasm but wondered whether others would, in that room that held no other visible ink. Was there something in our collective welcome, or lack thereof, that made that couple decide not to return? Those same questions often surface when our difference from others is evident, whether because of skin color, ethnicity, age, disability, gender identity, sexual orientation, or things like hair, clothing, and mannerisms. Will the church say *yes* to us, no matter how we appear?

Even if our difference is less evident, like some of the scars we considered in chapter 1, that difference can feel very prominent to us. We may enter with our shields up and radar activated, primed to notice the smallest slight or failing. A church perhaps cannot live up to those heightened sensitivities we bring with us.

But we who lead must own the responsibility to express welcome—a lavish *yes*—to people who come wondering whether the church can possibly offer that to them. This must include making this space holy for those who arrive unfamiliar with the people, the music, the behaviors, and the fellowship that will happen in our midst. It includes moving beyond a glib, smiling welcome to truly valuing those persons and what they bring with them—their perspectives, their gifts, and their experiences. The church changes with every new arrival. Henry Blackaby says, "I pay close attention to the people God adds to the body. Sometimes that is an indication of an assignment God is getting us ready for."[3] With each new arrival, some

---

2. This sentiment is oft-repeated. See generally Daniel, *Tired of Apologizing*; Evans, *Searching for Sunday*; Bolz-Weber, *Accidental Saints*, 10.

3. Blackaby and King, *Experiencing God*, 182.

of our long-held traditions and attitudes will have to give way so that the church can become what our increasing diversity enables us to be.

Behavior is sometimes an issue at the prison. We have loyal volunteers who know they're responsible for paying attention to what happens around the room. They deal gently but firmly with behavior that becomes disruptive. It sometimes feels clear that the problem isn't someone's desire to misbehave; it's her unfamiliarity with how we do things. What am I supposed to do while this singing happens? Seriously, are you telling me I can't eat this candy that I had in my pocket? Where do we line up for Holy Communion?

We begin every worship service with a good-natured reminder of the rules: no touching, no passing notes, no talking—unless, I sometimes say, it's to remark on what a good point Pastor Lee just made! Of course problems do happen, and occasionally a security officer has to be called. Usually a look or a word suffices to rein in the offense, and worship continues unimpeded.

Even in this setting where we offer a radical welcome, it surprises me how often a resident will express her frustration with some who have come for worship. "They're there for the wrong reasons," someone will say, airing her annoyance. "I stopped coming to church because I can't stand the cupcaking." In our prison, "cupcaking" means something like "meeting up with your girlfriend"—and these are not just platonic friendships. Worship is one of the places where women who live in different units can spend time together. It's true; they're not all there primarily to hear God's word. But why not welcome them anyway? "I hear you," I'll say. "Still, I'd rather they'd be here than out on the yard." Maybe something of what happens in worship will reach even that person who came for something else.

There are plenty of "wrong reasons" people go to church outside of the prison, too. Some young people come to church because their parents make them. Some reluctant adults attend because it's a priority for a loved one. I once had a parishioner I'll call Val who would show up with her two young daughters, but only when her mother was visiting. Val would greet me and others with great warmth and seeming familiarity, and I would welcome her with equal affection. It wasn't for me to let Val's mom know this happened only when she was in town!

One Sunday morning long before I went to the prison, I saw a woman pull into the church's parking lot, maybe half an hour before worship. She and her husband had been intermittently present in church, and I walked out to the entryway to greet her. I found her picking up a bulletin and turning to leave as she explained, flustered, that she couldn't stay but wanted to see what was going on that week. This was odd; this couple wasn't active in any of our mid-week offerings! That puzzling exchange became a little clearer when I answered a call the next day from the nearby men's work release center, asking whether this woman's husband had been in church. I'm pretty sure our worship service was on the stated agenda for this man's furlough from that community-based corrections facility. Picking up our bulletin was cover for whatever other activities he and his wife actually pursued that day. It was a reminder that people come to church—or don't!—for a lot of different reasons.

"Do you ever look down the row" in worship, I'll ask, "and think, 'That person doesn't belong here'?" I initiate this conversation dozens of times a year inside the prison, in the meetings I hold for women who want to be baptized. I ask each one to come to two meetings so that we can share our faith stories, learn about the meaning of baptism, and work our way through our baptismal ritual.

I always pause on the lengthy third question that asks if she will live out her baptism "in union with the church, which Christ has opened to persons of all nations, ages and races."[4] It's a great starting point for my question about the knee-jerk reactions we sometimes have to people sitting down the row from us in church. "I've done that, Pastor Lee," one of them will say. And she'll go on to describe a time when she thought someone didn't belong, based on what he was wearing, or how she acted, or the reason he had come that day. Someone else will chime in, agreeing that she, too, has been judgmental in that way.

This brings us back to those words of our ritual that remind us what's at stake in that reaction. "I think 'ages, nations and races' is a stand-in for a much longer list," I'll say. "The list could go on and talk about economic status, what kind of job you have, sexual orientation, gender identity, whether you're married or not, or have kids or not, your criminal history, and much more." I tell these sisters that I hope these ritual words—"the church which Christ has opened to persons of all nations, ages and races

4. See appendix 2.

53

[and more]"—will be echoing in our hearts when we start to get judgmental about the people who have wandered into church alongside us.

There's another, desperately important reason that I hope those words will take up residence in these sisters who so cheerfully come for baptism: "Sometimes," I'll say, "*we* may be the person that somebody looks at and says, 'She shouldn't be here.'" Heads nod as those words sink in. Some of them have already known the indignity and shame of a church that wouldn't welcome them. "I want you to remember *this* conversation," I say, looking around that room. "There's always a place for you in the church."

Is it true?

I believe, and I say with great earnestness to my sisters in prison, "There is a church that is *longing* to be gracious to you." I desperately hope I'm right. By "gracious" I mean welcoming, and also valuing, and living into relationship *with* her. I'll hasten to add that she may not find that church the first time she walks into one. If you don't, I'll say, then you can try calling those people to live up to this truth. But if they can't get there, or if you're not up to fighting that fight, then you shake the dust of that church off of your feet and go on to another. But don't give up on The Church.

I remember the church I was then attending, years ago, being gracious to a woman I'll call Jeannie who wandered in one Sunday. She was very needy. Jeannie showed up with her little girl and a list of things she needed. The relatively comfortable, goodhearted people of my church were glad to oblige, and that very week we found ourselves bringing diapers, toiletries, and some food to assist this little family.

The next week Jeannie came back, this time with a longer list. She could sure use some clothes because she was looking for a job and what she had wasn't suitable. It wasn't long before dresses, tops, and pants, size 12 or 14, started showing up, gleaned from members' closets, along with some shoes, underwear, socks, and more. Oh, and if any of us could give her a ride to those job interviews, that would be really helpful.

Week by week the list expanded. It soon included household items—a mattress, furniture, and some cleaning supplies—and intermittent child care. And a bit of money to help with utilities would take some pressure off, if we were willing to help that way.

It wasn't long before our collective goodness and welcome wore thin. Our outward friendliness grew strained, and our smiles calcified into resentment. Jeannie hadn't taken any of the jobs for which she had applied.

She seemed all too happy to rely on our goodness rather than doing the hard work of caring for herself and her young daughter. We felt she was taking advantage of us and we began to wonder how far we were expected to go in this relationship.

The next time a needy stranger walked into that church, our welcome was poisoned by that experience. Having gone too far with Jeannie, we naturally tended to wall ourselves off against the later Harry, or Juanita, or Darnell.

Decades later I heard the director of a homeless shelter wisely advise a bunch of volunteers: "Never work harder than the person you're trying to help."[5] I thought immediately of Jeannie. There was something wrong with the balance of effort in that episode. I thought of others through the years whom we were all too ready to help, but eventually found ourselves angry for having gone there.

It's a *rescuer* problem, according to Bill Selby, who says we are rescuers when we take "undue and excessive responsibility for the feelings, actions, and problems of another person." Taking on another person's stuff carries a huge emotional toll on us, and *it doesn't work* because, as Bill says, "Rescuing keeps the other in a victim position."[6]

The remedy for rescuing—and the associated drag on our favorable regard for other people—is good boundaries.[7] Boundaries remind us to take responsibility for what lies within our limits, and not to take on the things that belong to others. We can care, we can be supportive, and we can offer time, money, expertise, and other help as we feel called. But we must always understand and respect the limits of our responsibility, and grasp the possibility of caring about others without taking charge of what lies within *their* boundaries. This makes it possible to open ourselves to a relationship in which we can both be blessed.

Do these boundaries undo the *yes* that we talked about earlier? I don't think so. In fact, good, appropriate boundaries facilitate that *yes*; they make it possible! A church that does not have good boundaries will never be able

5. I am grateful to Tim Shanahan, director of Hawthorn Hill in Des Moines, Iowa (http://www.hawthorn-hill.org/), for this insight.

6. Bill Selby, "About Rescuing" (handout at workshop *Helping without Hurting*, Women at the Well UMC, Des Moines, March 19, 2016). Selby leads the Center for Pastoral Effectiveness of the Rockies. More information on Selby's programs can be found at http://www.pastoraleffectiveness.org/.

7. Cloud and Townsend, *Boundaries*, 27.

to let down its walls and offer a free and gracious welcome. Good boundaries are an integral element of a church set free to love well.

People often ask me how I stay well in my work as a pastor inside the prison. I'll answer by talking about taking days off, vacation, renewal leave, and my non-negotiable monthly massage, all of which are important. But eventually I'll get to the heart of the matter: *boundaries.*

I described in chapter 2 the limits on the help I'm allowed to offer residents at the prison. Living up to those rules is a matter of boundaries. If I were to let someone's need or friendship pull me past what I know I'm allowed to do, I would cross a boundary into an unhealthy space.

In the prison we live within dozens of boundaries, both physical and figurative. There are physical spaces the residents aren't allowed to enter; there are places they cannot be at all and others in which supervision is required. They can get in trouble for touching, talking too loud, sharing something they bought, showing up without an appointment, and quitting their jobs. I am seldom called upon to impose discipline for any of these infractions. But prison has taught me the importance of clear rules, consistently enforced.

It's the same lesson many of us had to learn as parents: Children do better when they know what is OK and what is not. The same is true for adults. I have learned to be unashamed in asking people to live up to the basic rules of behavior.

Boundaries are more than rule-enforcement tools. They're a means of protecting the *self* that we bring to the world. Boundaries keep us well. When I am clear on what is my responsibility and what is not, and give myself permission to tend to what is mine and let others do the same, we all become healthier.

For Christine this challenge arose with a dad who had cut off all contact. "I'm doing everything I can to make him proud of me," she said. Her list included substance abuse treatment, and her participation in Women at the Well, and she had just started going to book club once a week. "I want him to see that I've changed," she said, yearning. But when success seems to depend on someone else's reaction, I've learned to press: "Christine, what if he can't ever see it?" This is a boundaries question, and it turns our discussion to the deeper truth: Christine must work on being well, in herself, for her own well-being. Her wellness must not ultimately depend on whether her relationship with her father is restored.

The possibility of being well, in oneself, can stretch a person's imagination. I hear it often: "I can't imagine being well without having my _____ [my kids, my ex, my mom, my brother] in my life!" Well, you need to! Seriously, imagine it! Pause to wonder what wellness could possibly look like. And when you pursue that wellness in yourself, you'll find that's precisely what will best prepare you to be healthy in those other relationships. This truth seems always to come as a surprise. I'll sometimes quote the flight attendants' instruction to fasten your own oxygen mask first, before you assist the child or other person traveling with you. Quoting that teaching, I have been met with icy stares from women who have never flown on an airplane and who cannot imagine taking care of their own needs first. It's a lesson we would all do well to heed.

A church's resolve to eliminate walls and remain open and hospitable to all comers will paradoxically depend on good boundaries. We cannot maintain an increasingly diverse and welcoming space without some clarity on what belongs to each side of these new relationships.

Good boundaries will keep us from taking on too much of Jeannie's problems. They'll help us say what we're willing to do to help, and they'll help us clarify, unashamed, that there are things we won't do.

We may encounter behaviors that cross a line, and we will need to address them. By behaviors, I mean behaviors that happen in our midst, or within our community. This includes words and actions that impede programs, upend relationships, or manipulate people. When a person's behavior becomes disruptive to the worship or work we seek to do together, good boundaries will clarify what is permissible and what is not. Our community's life together depends on responding appropriately so that all may thrive. We'll explore in chapter 5 an example that illustrates this.

When I describe behaviors we need to address with good boundaries, I do not mean characteristics—even behavioral ones—that have to do with who we *are*. Healthy boundaries do not mean excluding people because we disagree with their political ideology, for instance, or their pregnancy out of wedlock, their sexual orientation, their family structure, or their economic condition. To do so would be to use the excuse of boundaries to erect the walls we have already said we must eliminate! We must be wise, and not reactionary and hidebound, in setting healthy boundaries.

———

I encourage women leaving prison to get at these boundary questions early in their connection with a church. Assuming she wants to do more than just sit in worship now and again, "sit down and talk with the pastor," I'll say, "or someone in leadership at that church. Tell them a bit of your story, including your stay in prison. Do it sooner rather than later." I don't love urging them to disclose these very personal details so early in that relationship. But the alternative seems much worse. Imagine a woman coming into a church and spending weeks and months getting connected with different groups and ministries. After some length of time, it somehow becomes known within that church that she was recently in prison. Persons who have spent time with her will feel confused and anxious: "She isn't who I thought she was." They'll think back over every encounter they've had with her: "Did she handle the offering?" "Was she alone with my children?"[8] They'll remember that she helped take Communion to the church's shut-ins; "Good grief, we sent a criminal into Mildred's apartment!"

Where the groundwork has been laid from the start of a person's connection with a church, and boundaries for that person's participation and perhaps supervision have been in place from the beginning, the later disclosure of a person's criminal history need not provoke such anxiety. The pastor or leadership team can—and must!—then stand up for her, calmly and graciously. "We knew about Sara's criminal record. We have been working with her since she arrived. We have an agreement about what she can do, and Jamal and Regina from our leadership team have been meeting with her and accompanying her when she's in the building." The specifics will vary case by case, and supervision will not be necessary in every case, but a measured, intentional process with appropriate limits is crucial. Otherwise, fear will likely shut down the welcome and openness we have fought so hard to achieve.

In some cases, a written covenant may be necessary, at least for a time. A clergy friend found herself writing just such a covenant when a young man, Jason, who had grown up in the church, was about to be released from prison on a sex offender charge. She obtained advice from various quarters and created a written agreement that was approved by her leadership group and shared with the church. It established the conditions for Jason to participate in the church's worship and programs. In that instance, he could

8. This answer should be "no" under Safe Sanctuary policies that would limit new members' access to children until after background checks have been completed. See Melton, *Safe Sanctuaries*. Guidelines and policies are also available at https://www.umc-discipleship.org/resources/safe-sanctuaries-general-guidelines-starter-documents.

attend only the Saturday evening service, when no children's programming occurred. Jason was to be accompanied by specified adults whenever he was on church grounds, and was not to use the restroom unattended. If he wanted to join in activities other than Saturday evening worship, he must ask permission ahead of time, which might or might not be granted, with or without conditions.

We may feel dismay at the idea of such narrow restrictions for a child of God to participate in the life of a church. I understand that concern. But there are consequences to our behavior; we as churches must take those seriously. Our underlying question must be: How will our welcome of this person allow him or her to enter into the life of the community? How will we be The Church with and for this individual? In a world with real consequences, how can we still recognize that she or he is a precious human being, called by God to be part of this community and, indeed, to enrich it with her or his presence? An example of a possible covenant that aims at that goal, with reciprocity and openness to change, is included in appendix 3.

Some of us may find unsettling the suggestion that a church would knowingly welcome a sex offender at all! Ex-cons, maybe, but someone on a sex offender registry? I have heard many stories of church leaders that demanded the exclusion of a sex offender without shame or apology. I cannot square that stance with the radical welcome Jesus offered. Sex offenders would have been among those at the table where Jesus ate dinner in Matthew 9. There Matthew, the tax collector whom Jesus has just called as a disciple, throws a dinner for Jesus and his followers. "Many tax collectors and sinners came and were sitting with him and his disciples" (Matt 9:10). The Pharisees notice what's happening and talk behind Jesus' back, asking his disciples why Jesus would do such a thing (9:11). When Jesus hears, he makes it clear that these are the people he's come for!

> "Those who are well have no need of a physician, but those who are sick. Go and learn what this means, 'I desire mercy, not sacrifice.' For I have come to call not the righteous but sinners" (Matt 9:12b–13).

These questions of radical welcome will stretch us if we take seriously Jesus' call for mercy. We don't get to exclude the sex offender nor the person who committed murder. We must be supportive of victims, but also of perpetrators. The details will look different in every circumstance, and we'll have to spend time and energy to work out our life together. But in The Church, both the welcome and the boundaries must be trustworthy and, as we'll see in chapter 5, we must have a meaningful plan to address conflict when it arises.

The Church is always open with no limits, and it expresses its welcome in part through healthy boundaries.

So how do we become churches that build boundaries, but not walls?

We start with "yes" where people are concerned. Our churches' answer to every human being must be *yes*. That's true for the person who has made her way into our parking lot or our church building, and it's true for the people we church folk meet out in the world.

Yes isn't our default setting with other human beings. We are well practiced in making instantaneous judgments all day long about who is safe, who is weird, who is sketchy, and whom we might ask for help. Sociology assures us that these judgments are natural, a survival strategy long engrained in us.[9] It's hard to offer the possibility of community with someone our instincts tell us we should avoid.

But the gospel calls us to more than our natural reaction! Jesus calls us to love. We really can practice smiling, extending a hand, and expressing genuine interest in other human beings. If I find myself balking at another person's behavior, it helps me to pause and wonder what memory this behavior is triggering in me, that it makes me so uncomfortable. I've also learned to wonder what might have happened to her, that she would act that way. Even if I don't know these answers, I find that asking the questions makes me more compassionate toward that person, and more insightful about my own discomfort

Brené Brown makes the case, in her excellent book *Rising Strong*, that, most of the time, most people are doing the best they can.[10] When we give people the benefit of the doubt, we begin to see them through God's eyes, in all their complexity and beauty. It is then that we can say *yes* and open the church, as the ritual says, "to persons of all ages, nations and races" and, by extension, of all quirks, failings, strengths, disabilities, histories, and circumstances. There must be no limits to our welcome of souls into the church community. As Pope Francis said: "I prefer a Church which is

9. Cleveland, *Disunity in Christ*, 46–51.
10. Brown, *Rising Strong*, chapter 6.

bruised, hurting and dirty because it has been out on the streets, rather than a Church which is unhealthy from being confined and from clinging to its own security."[11]

We make our rightful expectations and boundaries plain. Having welcomed them, we get to let people know what is expected of people who will be part of our faith community. I say "rightful" because we must be careful in deciding what those expectations are. When our expectations support the mission and welcome of the church, we rightfully call people to live up to them.

Churches would do well to invest some leadership time in these questions. What do we expect of persons who come into our building? Must they wear shoes and a shirt? What if they're under the influence, or they smell? What are the limits on loud or raucous behavior; do these things matter in our context, or under some circumstances? Are there steps we will take when we learn that a person was recently arrested, or released from prison, or on a sex offender registry? Having thought through these questions, at least among our leaders, we will be prepared to communicate these limits in an even-handed way, rather than reactively and hurriedly, caught off guard, which is likely to leave us closer to *no* than we mean to be.

To fail to address these questions is to demonstrate that we have no expectation of such a person ever entering our doors. That in turn becomes a self-fulfilling prophecy, and one that diminishes the community we seek to build within our churches.[12]

We practice a healthy, hospitable "no." If we set expectations and maintain boundaries, people will sometimes cross those lines. When that happens, we must be prepared to say "no." *No* may look like consequences that come into play because of what the person did. *No* may look like asking someone

11. Francis, *The Joy of the Gospel*, 25.

12. For an example of the kind of welcome that is possible when we think ahead of time about who might come to us, see the welcome statement adopted and posted by Custer Lutheran Fellowship in Custer, South Dakota: http://www.custerlutheran.com/about/welcome/.

to take accountability for what he or she did. It may look like exclusion from a particular role, or even from that particular church.[13]

I used to think that to be a Christian was to be a doormat. All that talk of love and hospitality and "kum ba yah"[14]: it seemed to communicate that we had to give and give until there was nothing left, and there was no room for our own needs and wellness to be respected.

I have long since abandoned that torturous understanding of our faith. Jesus asked us to love our neighbor *as we love ourselves* (Luke 10:27); we aren't required to give past the point of health and thriving. Jesus went apart from his followers and from needy crowds when he needed to pray; he took his disciples apart with him to rest.[15] Jesus said *no* to Peter, arguably his closest friend, when Peter couldn't accept Jesus' talk of what lay ahead in Jerusalem. "Get behind me, Satan!" Jesus cried (Mark 8:33; Matt 16:23). He said *no* when he needed to, and invites us to do the same.

We cannot be well in ourselves or as a church until we develop a faithful and honest "no." Practice it. Practice saying it without apology or shame. Sometimes the answer has to be "no." Not to who a person is—as we've discussed. Not to people having a place in The Church. But to maintain our rightful boundaries and care for our needs, individually and together, we must be able to say *no*.[16]

When *no* is necessary, let it be expressed in a healthy and hospitable way. Words like "no, I can't do that," or "no, that's against the rules," can be spoken evenly and matter-of-factly, and without the expectation that the person hearing them will respond with outrage or shame. Sometimes a *no* can be softened with a helpful alternative, or with a truthful explanation that helps to put that answer in perspective. "No, we can't let you sleep in the building. We've had some bad experiences with persons being here alone, and I'm unable to arrange someone to stay with you." Or, perhaps, to a returning citizen, "Our policy doesn't allow you to serve as an usher because of their role in collecting the offering. But our bell choir is looking for some new members." It is not helpful to argue or engage in endless

13. We discussed this possibility around domestic violence in chapter 3, at note 25 and accompanying text.

14. "Kum Ba Yah" is a well-known African American spiritual. Reprinted in United Methodist Publishing House, *UM Hymnal*, 120.

15. E.g., Mark 1:35, 6:30–32; Luke 5:16, 6:12; Matt 14:13, 23.

16. Many books and articles aim to help people do just this. Even WikiHow has a manual on this subject: https://www.wikihow.com/Say-No.

> *See, I am sending you out like sheep into the midst of wolves; so*
> *be wise as serpents and innocent as doves* (Matt 10:16).

Jesus sends his newly chosen disciples out into the towns and villages to "proclaim the good news" (Matt 10:7), "cure the sick, raise the dead, cleanse the lepers," and "cast out demons" (10:8a). He offers a packing list for what they may carry, and instructions for where they may stay. And then he says the ominous words quoted above. Suddenly we grasp that this will be a dangerous mission. They may face persecution. Fear will arise—but it must not consume them (10:28).

From this very earliest missionary journey, hazards threatened. If we're going to walk into uncharted territory, we may find ourselves at risk. In guiding them through that, Jesus said. "Be wise as serpents and innocent as doves" (10:16b). By this he means: Be shrewd and pay attention to what is going on around you. Don't bumble your way into traps. Use your best skills; negotiate wisely. At the same time, though, be "innocent." Be always above reproach. Don't give anyone an excuse to accuse you of wrongdoing.

I've shared this advice countless times with women trying to make their way through the challenges of prison life. There's great wisdom for us, too, outside the prison, as we tear down walls and create wise boundaries. How might you be served by actions that are at once cunning and blameless?

debate. Give the level of explanation that is appropriate, without flinching, and take whatever next step is required.

Often, we wait too long. Jasper comes into our church, looking ragged. Instead of addressing him, Alyce turns to Jo, eyebrows raised, and they have a conversation punctuated by uneasy glances in his direction. One of them might go and summon a staff member. Anxiety increases, and perhaps shame, and Jasper begins to get the message that he is not welcome. By the time anyone addresses him directly, the hope of a meaningful relationship has faded. How much better when we prepare ourselves and one another to meet strangers with kindness and warmth? If upon initiating a conversation graciously we discover that Jasper is in need, or poses a threat, we can say the appropriate *yes* or *no* grounded in love.

Finally, we'll need to take care that our *no* is applied evenhandedly. It would be easy to create boundaries that get enforced only when people who are "different" cross them. If we indulge Trudy with a *yes* we won't offer to LeBron, or vice versa, under identical circumstances, we have not practiced boundaries fairly.

A good practice of saying *no* will protect the broad and generous *yes* we offer with walls down. It will keep relationship first, rather than programs, as we discussed in chapter 2. And it will keep us aligned with Jesus' commandment that we love one another. Imagine a *no* that can be expressed *and received* in love and with respect. It's possible; I've seen it! We'll talk more about that in chapter 5.

Questions:

a. Take an honest look at your church's space, its signs, programs, activities (including worship), and communications. Literally, walk through your space and look at everything, including your bulletin boards, what gets projected on your walls, and who gets pictured in your publicity. What is being expressed about who is welcome and who is not? Who belongs, and who doesn't? What "walls" surround your church?

b. How is your church's openness balanced with good boundaries? What are the explicit or implicit expectations for behavior and for the well-being of persons in your church? Are those expressed in loving and welcoming ways? Can they be?

c. What are your personal boundaries around your care for others? Can you say "no" when you need to? Do you worry that people will take advantage of your kindness? How can healthy boundaries help you love yourself and love your neighbor?

d. How is a church strengthened when forbidding walls are replaced with healthy boundaries? What keeps us from pursuing this goal? What would Jesus do?

e. Name one or two specific steps you will take to eliminate walls and/ or to erect healthy boundaries. What do you need to practice? What resources might help you in this work?

5

The Church Brings Its Messes
into the Light

What have we done? What have we done to our siblings?
Hear their blood cry, hear their blood cry from the blessed earth
What have we done? What have we done to our siblings?
O God, have mercy on us Oh oh oh

—RICHARD BRUXVOORT COLLIGAN[1]

From the very first time I participated in a meeting of Women at the Well's inside council, this group of eight to eighteen women began to teach me what I have come to believe our churches need to know about accountability and reconciliation.

I was still on my way to becoming the pastor there; I was shadowing my predecessor, Pastor Arnette, as a way of getting oriented. I remember Arnette being pleased that I would be there for the inside council meeting that afternoon. The inside council is made up of residents who choose to come to meetings, and keep coming and, after attending five consecutive meetings, face a vote on whether they will become full members. I often laugh with leaders of churches outside the prison who say, "If that's how *our*

1. Bruxvoort Colligan, "Lament," verse 4 (lyrics based on Gen 4:10).

65

council worked, we wouldn't have one!" Whether it's the five consecutive meetings or getting through the vote, they have a point.

In that very first meeting, I was stunned when one member, Connie, publicly apologized to another, Jenny, for seizing an opportunity that she knew Jenny had wanted, to represent Women at the Well on the institution's religious advisory committee. Jenny accepted Connie's apology and the two exchanged words of appreciation and friendship.

I remember thinking I had never witnessed anything like this. The agenda for that meeting actually included time for members to clear the air, when there was friction between them. This was new and uncharted territory. And I had just watched it happen *in prison*: the place I least expected peace.

In my lifelong experience in churches outside the prison, I knew how messes are typically addressed. Lana will do something that angers someone, or several someones. The aggrieved parties will talk about it among themselves, or with their friends, but Lana will be left out of that conversation, except for the occasional muttering that Lana will pretend she didn't hear. Friends will line up with outrage or support on both sides of the issue. Sometimes these situations will blow over without much ado. Sometimes they will make their way to the church's leadership group with a request for a new set of guidelines against the perceived offense. Too often, the aggrieved parties—or the now-shunned Lana—will decide to look for a different church.

I have seen this pattern play out in all kinds of disputes. It might be about who manages what in the church kitchen, or who gets to add new names to the usher list. It might involve who will sing during the special anniversary service, or how the memorial money gets spent, or whether to spend the money to resurface the parking lot. Maybe it's a new vision statement, or funding for that outreach program, or offering space to that Congolese congregation. We make a lot of decisions and undertake a lot of activity in the local church. There are plenty of things to argue about.

Nothing in this typical pattern involves a plan or expectation for Lana and the persons who feel wronged to address the issue in a meaningful way within that church, or even within its leadership team, with the goal of correction and reconciliation. We rarely ask how the original relationship can be mended. It becomes generally known that *these* persons won't work with *those*. We might tell new folk, ruefully, "Oh, don't mind Lana; she's a little hard to take." We settle for repeatedly diminished expectations in which relationships within the church are less honest and more fractured than they were meant to be. We haven't even noticed that we fall short of a higher ideal, because we have lost track of that possibility.

For us inside the prison, practicing peace is not optional. In most churches, if you have a dispute with someone, you can go home and to work and get on with your week. Most of us won't have to deal with that troublesome person until next Sunday or, at worst, the mid-week committee meeting or prayer group. By contrast, prison is a 24–7 enterprise where you are going to bump into that adversary over and over, in church services and dining hall, at work and in that program you're both taking. You'll see each other in the yard, or down the hall in the living unit where you both reside, or even in the room you share. Residents can rarely nurse a hurt privately, and every aspect of prison life invites amplification of the drama and division that arise between people. The I-just-need-to-vent conversation with someone you thought you could trust too often ends in disclosure, betrayal, and one more proof that you simply can't trust anybody.

The intensity of life together means that our leaders know each other better than leaders do in many outside churches. They scrutinize one another in a variety of settings, and not just in the relatively rarefied context of worship and meeting time. I sometimes become the repository of complaints by one leader against another, based on her conduct at work or in their living unit, more often than anything that happens in the Sacred Place. In one rocky season, there wasn't a single person on our council about whom I hadn't heard a complaint from someone else in the group.

In such a context, in order to do life together as a church, we have to address head-on the issues among us. Our approach starts with Jesus' words in Matthew 18:

> If another member of the church sins against you, go and point out the fault when the two of you are alone. If the member listens to you, you have regained that one. But if you are not listened to, take one or two others along with you, so that every word may be confirmed by the evidence of two or three witnesses. If the member refuses to listen to them, tell it to the church; and if the offender refuses to listen even to the church, let such a one be to you as a Gentile and a tax collector. Truly I tell you, whatever you bind on earth will be bound in heaven, and whatever you loose on earth will be loosed in heaven. (Matt 18:15–18)

This teaching is formalized in our council membership expectations, which we distribute to and discuss with every new attendee.[2] With the high turnover within our prison population, we have not tried to bring the congregation as a whole into this process, even though Jesus seems to contemplate that happening. So far it has been enough to seek to live out these words by making them the guidelines for our council.

These rules accomplish several very important things. First, they establish that peace among members of our council is of primary importance. Part of our witness as a congregation, both with residents inside the prison and with volunteers and guests outside, comes from the peace and community that prevails among our leaders. We don't just speak of welcome, love, and forgiveness; we *expect* it.

Second, our guidelines offer a way forward through the untidy thickets of interpersonal disputes. When an issue arises between two members, our guidelines lay out what is supposed to happen. One person is to go to the other and seek to resolve it. If that doesn't succeed, she is to bring one or two others from the council along to have a further conversation. If it remains unresolved, they are invited to bring me, their pastor, into it. If the issue still remains, we discuss it at a council meeting. It's a clear process with specific steps, all aimed at bringing resolution and peace.

Third, these written expectations keep me from being the referee and enforcer among members of our council. When someone comes with a complaint about another member, she often hopes that I'll step in and take care of the issue. To do so would involve me in an unhealthy triangle, when the issue needs to remain between these two women.[3] Instead, I've learned to ask whether she has worked the process. Sometimes I'll pull out the document and remind her how it's supposed to work. The question usually arises: Is it worth it to her to follow through? If it is, great, and we'll bring it to the full council if it goes that far. If it's not—and it often isn't—it helps put things into perspective. "It's not that big of a deal," she might say. And I'll state the corollary: "If that's true, then let it go, and don't let this stand in the way of your relationship."

Finally, the guidelines make it clear: This work belongs to our council. The women involved share their versions of what has happened, and members talk to one another. As their pastor, I might offer some reminders about the rules or remind them to keep the conversation civil. But ultimately the

2. See appendix 4.

3. See, e.g., Cloud and Townsend, *Boundaries*, 133–35.

discussion belongs to the sisters around that table, those who live together and lead this church. *They* are the ones whose relationships matter; *they* are the ones with wisdom about truth-telling and accountability and what is needed to restore trust. I am humbled by the care and commitment that is evident as we live this process.

All of this is intense and often painful. Life experience has taught some of our members that difficult conversations lead to rage, violence, and trauma. Even when issues are addressed in a civil and measured way, anxiety surges and some will withdraw. Yet the stakes are high, and in pressing on, we help one another see that we can disagree safely and remain in relationship. "This is critically important work that we're doing here," I'll say. "We could stop talking and pretend like everything is OK, but it's not yet, and we have to trust that we can get there." Again and again, we do.[4]

In all my years in churches outside the prison, I haven't been part of any comparable process aimed at addressing and restoring relationships. Matthew 18, quoted above, sometimes gets lifted up as the method a church will follow. But it's rarely practiced openly. We in the local church have long been encouraged to establish an intentional faith development process in order to grow discipleship among our people.[5] What if an intentional relationship restoration process came to be viewed as equally essential? The call to love our neighbor is at the heart of discipleship (Luke 10:27). What does it say about our faithfulness when we cannot stay in loving relationship with the people right next to us, in our own local churches?

It saddens me particularly when I become aware of friction among leaders—including clergy leaders—in local churches. Those stories are not uncommon, of lead and associate pastors, or of pastors and lay leaders, who have become aloof and divided among themselves. How can we lead worship together authentically, and provide pastoral leadership to a church,

---

4. Desmond Tutu and Mpho Tutu emphasize this in their *Book of Forgiving* (24): "This is what healing demands. Behavior that is hurtful, shameful, abusive, or demeaning must be brought into the fierce light of truth. And truth can be brutal. In fact, truth may exacerbate the hurt; it might make things worse. But if we want real forgiveness and real healing, we must face the real injury."

5. See, e.g., Rainer and Geiger, *Simple Church*, chapter 5. The development of a discipleship pathway in every church has been named a "Wildly Important Goal" for the Iowa conference of the United Methodist Church. See https://www.iaumc.org/wildlyimportantgoal.

as teams that have allowed that "root of bitterness" to spring up in us (Heb 12:15)?

It is a matter of some pride for me that in the nearly eight years my husband and I led a church together as co-pastors, before I went to Women at the Well, he and I never once walked into worship without first coming to a place of peace around whatever issues might have arisen between us, personally or professionally. We sometimes stood in that conference room near the entrance to the sanctuary, gazing wearily at one another and wondering whether this would be the week that we couldn't reach a resolution. But peace was a priority for both of us, and this was where the rubber hit the road. One of us would manage to utter some words that would break the logjam. We would acknowledge to one another that it would be OK. Somehow we would be able to express our reconciliation, with a hug and usually a kiss, more than once just in time to enter the sanctuary together to begin worship.

The most severe test of our inside council's commitment to accountability and reconciliation came a few years ago when one member, Krystal, repeatedly became the subject of conversation during the time in our agenda for addressing issues among members. Krystal had long been a dear and loyal member of Women at the Well and literally every program we offered: our choir, our council, every small group, and any special gathering. But over time, she began to consume a huge amount of our council's time and energy.

It started when it became clear that she wasn't living up to the expectation of confidentiality about the conversations we hold in our council meetings. Other council members would hear her, in their shared living unit, talking about a difficult subject that was discussed in our meeting earlier that day. They would bring that concern to her, and eventually to a meeting, and Krystal would apologize and be offered forgiveness. And then it would happen again.

Pretty soon a new problem surfaced: Krystal was stirring up dissension among members of the council. She would tell a member about a decision made at a meeting that member had missed, but she would do so in a way that was hurtful, or that misstated what had happened. Much unnecessary and messy friction ensued, with more council time being devoted to Krystal and her issues. We would have an agenda full of work we wanted to do together, and our scheduled time would draw to an end with nearly all of the time used in what became known as *the Krystal discussion*. "I wasn't trying to hurt anyone," she would say. That may have been true, but it wasn't enough. "You've got to try *not* to hurt anyone," one of her sisters would respond.

After a few months of frustration and disappointment for us all—including Krystal—and many hours I spent with Krystal, hoping she could see how to do better, we scheduled a time in which council members who wanted to speak about these issues could do so. The goal was to encourage Krystal, clarify facts, and discern whether she could live up to what was required of her to remain a council member. Krystal was invited to bring a support person to that meeting, to sit with her and hear what was said.

I will never forget the conversation we had that day. Eight or nine council members crowded into that small conference room, and each woman had her say. Krystal listened as each one described the effect of Krystal's actions: how this sister had been hurt, or how a relationship had been damaged. It was a remarkable gathering, in that each one offered her thoughts with an evident desire to be absolutely clear, but without rancor or a desire to blame or shame Krystal. In this gathering, I saw The Church, "speaking the truth in love" (Eph 4:15).

As our time together drew to a close, someone asked Krystal whether she thought she could stop doing these hurtful things. She responded with a very honest "I don't know." We prayed and adjourned.

And at our council meeting the following week, one of our members made a motion that Krystal's membership on the council be terminated. After a short discussion, there was a vote, the motion passed, and Krystal walked out of the room.

I hope you can hear in these words that this was a wrenching decision. It wasn't an outcome any of us wanted. But it was the *right* thing, and we did it the right way. How do I know that? First, it was the right thing, because so long as Krystal remained on the council, her presence was damaging the relationships we work so hard to build there. Equally important, time spent on *the Krystal discussion* kept us from pursuing other business. A couple of meetings after Krystal was removed, we made our way through a full agenda and one member observed, "It has been so long since we did that!" She was right. Dealing with our messes allows the church's work to move forward.

Second, I know we did this in the right way—though perhaps more slowly than some would have liked—because, through it all, *Krystal stayed connected.* Many of us wouldn't have. We would have taken our toys and gone home to nurse our hurt and anger. But Krystal dared to come back to nearly all our activities, throughout the next year while she remained in prison. I am certain that happened in part because, after she left the group that had just voted her out, the council had a conversation about how to deal with Krystal now. "She can't be a member of the council, but she's still a member of the church," we said. Members talked about how important it would be for them to greet Krystal out in the yard, and speak to her if they were in her living unit. She needed to know she still had a place in the church, even if her gifts did not fit her as a leader. I watched as all that became true, and Krystal was able to become *dear* again, once her mischief was ended.

The church in the world has been tainted by media reports of the persistent problem of misconduct that happens there. Child sexual abuse within the Catholic Church is perhaps the most widely publicized of these, but sexual misconduct occurs in all traditions and is not just against children. Financial wrongdoing is similarly a chronic problem within the church that grabs headlines and damages the communities where it occurs. Misconduct can involve persons in many different roles within our churches, and is particularly injurious when it involves paid staff, and especially clergy leaders.

These very serious wrongs are beyond the scope of this book. Our denominations and judicatories offer various processes to resolve allegations of misconduct, often by decision-makers at an institutional level far from the local church. It is worth noting that the local church remains the locus for much of the fallout from those distant decisions; disciplinary decisions will deeply affect individuals and their multi-layered relationships with one another. Do we have a plan for seeking resolution among these people who were most directly affected by someone's wrongdoing? What does reconciliation look like for them, and within the local church? Could the process I describe in this chapter be useful in those cases? Loose ends left untended can unsettle a church for decades. I fear this is another instance in which we settle for less than loving, gracious community. Instead we linger in a kind of uneasy civility—if that—in the wake of misconduct within our congregation.

There are a lot of messes in the church that we seem to have no plan or intention to clean up fully.

We've already talked about how our council at the prison deals with interpersonal issues. A companion provision addresses misconduct. If a member is found guilty on a "major"—a major disciplinary ticket—she is expected to share about it with the group as a way of addressing the wrong she has thereby committed against the inside council as a whole. Every time we meet, our agenda leaves room for the question: Are there any membership issues or majors we need to discuss? It's a way of bringing our messes into the light, with intentionality and without surprise. Most majors become known across the prison yard anyway. If a member emerges from a disciplinary process and the issue is never discussed within our circle, it can become the elephant in the room.

We have discussed majors that are as simple as Erma placing a phone call to her boyfriend who was on parole. Contact with another felon is prohibited unless an exception is made, and Erma had not yet received an answer on her request for that permission. Cindy's major had to do with possessing other people's clothing, taken during her job in laundry. Darlene, in a wheelchair and assisted by another offender who served as her aide, received a major for assaulting that aide with her walker.

When one of our leaders reports on her major, we talk it through. There is typically a general reaction that has to do with how serious this infraction seems to be, and how it reflects on Women at the Well. Our leaders take very seriously the privilege of being connected with this ministry, and when one of our number gains attention for her misconduct, that act is perceived to reflect on all of us.

So, for instance, an assault on an aide is a much more serious matter than an errant phone call, and our leaders aren't afraid to say so. Darlene might be asked to write an essay and bring it to the next meeting to share how this happened, and to reflect on who—including our ministry—was harmed by her actions.

In every conversation about wrongdoing, the council is keenly interested in whether the offending sister takes responsibility and is sorry for her actions. Cindy seemed sincerely mystified by the circumstances that led her to take those items of clothing. She expressed shock and remorse and her friends believed her.

Even when an infraction is perceived to be minimally serious, like that phone call, I have been impressed and moved by the care with which some council members will address the situation. The broken rule may not particularly reflect on our ministry, or on that sister's status as a council member. Still, our long-standing member Sarah might offer some well stated counsel: "I hope you'll think about whether it was worth breaking the rules." Having a major on your record can negatively affect housing, privileges, and parole decisions. "It's not a bad thing to learn to wait until you had permission. You'll do better in life if you can wait," Sarah will go on. And then in the knowing way of women in prison concerning the men in their lives, Sarah might wink and say, "He's probably not worth it anyway."

Maybe this Matthew 18 business is all well and good for women in prison, where everyone is already a known rule-breaker, and maybe it's great that we're able to manage that there. But is it realistic outside? Will the people in your local church engage in conversations like the ones I've described?

It may be a stretch. After all, we have a reputation to uphold within our churches and in our communities. We're *respectable*. Who among us would submit ourselves and our wrongs to a bunch of peers and let them talk to us as if their opinion matters?

You may be right; we may not let ourselves go there. But if that's true, it's sad how little we trust one another, and how much we feel we have to hide in order to be part of a church community. It's also worth wondering why we trust so little in the process Jesus himself gave us. This isn't *my* idea; it's right out of the Bible! Perhaps an illustration is in order, of how this might work.

Let's say you're a social drinker and one night you get stopped on the highway after one too many beers. What you thought would be a speeding ticket turns into an OWI (operating while intoxicated), and you're a little embarrassed. You feel found out, and you're a little worried that your drinking is getting out of hand.

In the typical church, you aren't going to talk about your OWI. When you walk into that building again, you might wonder if someone saw your car stopped there on the side of the road. You might check whether OWI tickets get published somewhere, and wonder if some sanctimonious person here has looked at that list. When you see some of your fellow leaders glance in your direction and then laugh together, you may wonder, "Do they know?" But you say nothing, and they say nothing, and you go on with your various church roles without really knowing, and with no way to clear the air on the subject. There is no correction; there are no words of grace. But what isn't said colors everything that happens that day, and a long time after.

Now imagine with me that your church's leadership group has a regular time on the agenda for airing disputes among its members and addressing wrongs they report to the group. You won't be very excited about showing up for that meeting, the week after your OWI ticket. But you go anyway, and when that time comes in the meeting, you shakily raise your hand.[6] You tell about the ticket, take responsibility for it, and ask forgiveness.

Someone sitting there might say, "My teenage daughter drove with some friends to a movie that night, and you know we live on the same highway you do. How could you drive drunk and put those kids at risk?" Another member might say, "You know you could always call me if you need a designated driver." Someone else might observe, "The time I got an OWI it was a huge wake-up call. I started going to AA. I was mad about the ticket, but it was the best thing that could have happened."

As these words unfold, your reactions will contribute to the exchange as you maybe thank one person for their words, and as you admit that you hadn't thought about those kids and who else might be at risk. You might become able to acknowledge some of your feelings and hear words of connection, affirmation, and encouragement. Along the way, someone will say, "Thank you for being honest about what happened." And you will walk out of that room feeling supported and connected to people who know more about you and love you anyway.

At least that's what will happen if the process works the way it should. It's what happens in an AA meeting, right? One is likely to feel both challenged and supported. I am grateful to AA for modeling this stance, yet it saddens me to acknowledge that our churches have not always been trustworthy to offer that same gift to those who dare to tell their truths.

It is perhaps a risky proposition. We may worry that what we say in church could backfire. "I can't tell what I did; it will get used against me in court!" Even if there are sometimes limits on what we can appropriately say, and times when our confession must be limited to a pastoral confidence, must we not still find ways to share our truth, to be held accountable, to seek reconciliation, and to renew our relationships?

---

6. It may be easier to imagine this happening with a staff team or a small group or covenant group. Even if this process could occur only in those more limited settings, that effort would represent a step toward transparency in many churches.

Now take a moment and imagine the scenario we just considered, but this time it's the pastor who is the guilty party. Does that make a difference as you imagine the conversation among church leaders? Should it?

These questions press toward Howard Zehr's concept of restorative justice. In contrast our current system of retributive justice that sees crime as "a violation of the state, defined by lawbreaking and guilt," restorative justice redefines crime as "a violation of people and relationships" that "creates obligations to make things right."[7] Zehr fleshes out these obligations by asking six questions:

1. Who has been hurt?
2. What are their needs?
3. Whose obligations are these?
4. What are the causes?
5. Who has a stake in this situation?
6. What is the appropriate process to involve stakeholders in an effort to address causes and put things right?[8]

Our criminal justice system fails to address most of these questions.

The process Jesus offers in Matthew 18 invites the church to be a place where things *can* be set right. Zehr's questions will naturally come up when we have the conversations Jesus invites. It won't be easy; even Zehr acknowledges this all sounds rather hopelessly utopian![9] But I am not so jaded as to believe this is impossible, and I urge all of us who claim the gospel to trust that Jesus knew what he was talking about. The shallow community that exists within many of our churches today is not the fullness to which we are called.

I must admit that none of this works perfectly inside the prison, either. There are women who stop coming to council meetings at a time when they would otherwise need to discuss a major. We have lost members who couldn't stomach another member's presence but weren't willing to go through the reconciliation process we have covenanted to follow. While that saddens me, I am convinced that our process remains correct; it produces a community of leaders who are, for the most part, at peace with one another week by week for our formal gatherings as well as when they meet one another on the grounds of the prison.

7. Zehr, *Changing Lenses*, 183.
8. Ibid., 237.
9. Ibid., 227.

Anything less falls short of what it means to be leaders in the first place. I have been part of too many leadership groups in which disagreement is discouraged, and members do not feel able to discuss the real issues that divide us. Behind that experience are often instances in which other leaders shamed us or made us fearful of asserting our voices and opinions. That, too, is a mess that a healthy church will address and root out, so that on issues of whatever magnitude, we grow into a body of leaders in which "iron sharpens iron" (Prov 27:17) and we are clothed always in love (Col 3:14).

The church responds to misbehavior and division with intentional movement toward accountability, resolution, and renewed relationship.

So how do we become churches that bring our messes into the light?

We speak the truth in love. We are often better at speaking truth than expressing love. We can share facts and details, but does it come from a place of caring and support? In the world—especially in the political arena—we can now expect speech that is angry and one-sided. In church, we are called to speak the truth, to acknowledge when there's another side to the story, and to say only what we're sure of. And we're called to speak that truth with love.

Can any of us honestly say that our words are spoken from a place of authentic care for the other person? It's hard! Go back and read the Apostle Paul's description of love in First Corinthians 13: Who can live up to a kind of love that "is not envious or boastful or arrogant or rude" (13:4–5a)? Who can love without being irritable or resentful (13:5)? Can we bear all things, believe all things, hope all things, and endure all things (13:7)? We may not be able to fully manage any of these things, but something important happens when we keep that aim before us.

I see it in our inside council conversations, especially as they end. Once it is clear whether the council views an infraction as a big issue or a small one, and any consequences have been decided, a moment comes when the mood softens and words of support are offered. "We've all been there, sister," Karen might say. "Please don't beat yourself up about it." Someone else might say, "You've already been punished enough," after hearing about the days served in solitary confinement, or the privileges that were lost. Even where significant doubt exists about the member's ability to resolve the situation, there are words of grace. "Honey, we want you to succeed in this." The overall message upon ending these discussions is that she is still a valued part of the community, still part of us, and that we as a group are holding hope for her to come back from whatever happened.

We aren't afraid to impose consequences. This section is reminiscent of the healthy, hospitable *no* we discussed in chapter 4. If I've just received an OWI, I need to be taken off the list of adults that drive the youth to their events, and the other leaders of the church shouldn't have to feel any compunction about imposing that consequence. Consequences, like boundaries, aren't about making one another feel bad. They're limits that need to be in place to keep persons safe. A new church member recently released from prison shouldn't be surprised when she is asked not to handle the offering, any more than a person with a communicable disease might be asked to step out of the kitchen for now.

Consequences are for the good of the community, but also for the person whose actions prompted them. The speeding ticket my son earned on the way home from school, shortly after obtaining his permit, made the roads safer for other drivers, yes, but it also changed the way he looked at speeding. He became a better and safer driver because an officer impressed upon him how little was to be gained, and how much could be lost, by failing to observe the speed limit. We all become healthier when consequences are imposed fairly and consistently.

Consequences are the results that logically flow from something that has happened, for good reason, and without a punitive intent. The OWI charge and fine cover the punishment for that behavior; now the question for the church is what consequences need to be in place to limit risk and to respond appropriately. Appropriate consequences, fairly imposed, for a reasonable period, will help us in our quest for accountability, resolution, and renewed relationship.

We don't settle for the appearance of peace. I remember a church member who once talked about the difference between "false community" and "true community."[10] False community is what you have when people are nice on

10. A summary of these ideas can be found at Greenfield, "Four Stages of Community";

the surface and don't address the truth of what is going on underneath. It's the church where rumors and anger abound but are never addressed. True community is what you reach once you tackle the rumors and get to the bottom of them, and figure out whether anger is justified and what to do about it. True community emerges when a person can stop hiding the truth about herself and discover that she can still be valued, can still contribute her gifts, and can have an ongoing role in a community that wants her to be there. True community is what happens when we get past the appearance of peace to a place of *actual* peace, what Martin Luther King Jr. called the beloved community,[11] where we put down our swords for good.

At the heart of all this is *forgiveness*. Are we willing to hold one another accountable and offer forgiveness when that is due, or aren't we? In their excellent *Book of Forgiving*, Bishop Desmond Tutu and his daughter Mpho offer a fourfold path toward forgiveness: "1. Telling the story. 2. Naming the hurt. 3. Granting forgiveness (recognizing shared humanity). 4. Renewing or releasing the relationship."[12] We can choose to walk this path instead of following "the revenge cycle" that endlessly and fruitlessly moves through pain and harm, revenge and cruelty.[13]

Forgiveness is not for the faint of heart. It is hard work. Bishop Desmond and Mpho remind us that forgiveness is a muscle that we need to exercise; the more practice we have, the stronger we will be.[14] This is true whether we're offering forgiveness to others, or asking for it when we offend someone else, or when we need to forgive ourselves for our own errors.

Where better than the church to hone and strengthen this muscle? Forgiveness is at the heart of our theology, our talk about God. It must also be at the center of our ministry, in terms of how we welcome, teach, worship, lead, and grow together as disciples of Jesus Christ. The church where those things are happening offers something the world needs more than it knows. It's not too much to say that forgiveness has the capacity to change the world.[15]

Peck, *Different Drum*.

11. An introduction to King's idea of the "beloved community" can be found at King Center, "The King Philosophy."

12. Tutu and Tutu, *Book of Forgiving*, 49.

13. Ibid.

14. This statement appears under "Today's Challenge," at Day 1 of the thirty-day online *Tutu Global Forgiveness Challenge*. "Forgiveness is a muscle, and it helps to train on the smaller weights before you attempt to pick up the giant barbell." https://www.forgivenesschallenge.com.

15. Tutu and Tutu, *Book of Forgiving*, 219.

> *Nothing is covered up that will not be uncovered, and nothing secret that will not become known. What I say to you in the dark, tell in the light; and what you hear whispered, proclaim from the housetops.* (Matt 10:26b–27)
>
> Jesus' speech that we considered in chapter 4, as he sent his disciples into a challenging world, includes these words, too. What is secret right now, he says, won't be for long. Nothing will remain covered up; everything secret will become known.
>
> Our life experience may not prove that to be true. It seems that far too many truths remain buried, far too long. But the movement of God clearly is toward uncovering and unearthing. "The truth will make you free," Jesus says in another place (John 8.32b). Again and again, strength and healing are found in the disclosure of the truth even when it is hard.

Questions:

a. Can you recall some times when your church has held someone accountable for his or her misbehavior? Was there a meaningful and peaceful resolution? Why or why not? Are there times when persons have misbehaved and not been called to account? How has the brokenness in relationships affected your church's witness to your community?

b. Does your church have an intentional process—explicit or implicit—for resolving conflict? Do leaders and members know what it is? Is it implemented regularly? What values does it express? How does the use or disuse of this process communicate the importance of accountability in your church?

c. How do you personally experience conflict and forgiveness in your relationships? Do you regularly demand accountability and work toward resolution? Or do you settle for less than your original expectations? Why or why not? Do you take accountability when you are the offending party? How do you know when forgiveness has been reached?

d. How is a church strengthened when misbehavior is not simply tolerated? What values are expressed when we hold one another accountable and seek resolution and renewed relationship? Are we worried about destroying relationships by naming misbehavior? What could be the good outcomes of holding people accountable?

e. Name one or two situations where you need to hold someone accountable, and make a plan for doing so in love. If you are in a relationship poisoned by unforgiveness, think of some ways you might move toward peace with one another. What would it take to believe that you don't have to settle for the brokenness between you?

6

The Church Has Something Critically Important to Offer

welcome to this circle where love and grace abound
we honor your journey and wherever you are bound
we will walk beside you encourage you on your way
celebrate your spirit and hold you as we pray

there is love for one like you
there is grace enough to see you through
and wherever you have walked
whatever path you choose
may you know there is love for one like you

—TRISH BRUXVOORT COLLIGAN[1]

One evening Lauren came by my office, with a look that signaled she needed to talk. I had gotten to know her a little bit in the preceding months. She seemed a placid soul, a little cautious.

She had told me that the first night she came to worship, I dipped my hand in the water of the baptismal font, which stands at the back of the

1. Bruxvoort Colligan, "Welcome to This Circle."

sanctuary. We fill it and invite our worshippers to touch the water as they come forward for communion. That night she says I waved my wet hand and spattered water onto the women nearby, which included Lauren, as I said, "Remember your baptism and be thankful." "That meant a lot to me," Lauren told me, more than once. "I hadn't remembered it for a very long time."

That evening when we sat down together, Lauren explained that it was the anniversary of her crime, and she wanted to talk about what happened. She had never been able to talk about it out loud. And then she told it all, of the drugs she had been on, and the child she was caring for, and the crying that just wouldn't stop, until she lost control. Lauren told this terrible story for the first time and, after a pause, I drew out more of what had happened in her life, including the mom that started giving her heroin when she was a third grader, and the father—followed by a string of boyfriends—who had abused her.

As Lauren's words ran out, I didn't have many, either. We talked about forgiveness. We talked about the worst thing we've ever done not having the power to define us, even if it will define where we live, as it did then for Lauren. We prayed together and Lauren left having experienced the heart of church: welcome, truth, forgiveness, belonging.

I wonder if we've lost track of why church *matters*. Do we believe that the church has something critically important to offer the world? Can we explain that belief to someone who doesn't know it? Or do we participate in church with a bit of sheepishness?

"Sure, I love those church potlucks," we might say. And we might mean it, in spite of the inevitable ham balls, the green Jell-O, the six-ounce water glasses, and the mediocre coffee that feel outdated in today's culture. We mean it, some of us, because there remains something holy in sitting at table together, as we share stories and laughter. The church has always found ways for us to become known to one another, with bonds of fellowship that connect us in love. I *know* that; I'll even admit that I enjoy a ham ball from time to time! But I don't always find the words to tell someone else that truth.

Potlucks are a rather dated example of the long list of gifts our churches offer. What gifts are you ready to claim: Music that brings tears unbidden? The perfume that lingers after someone's embrace? The passion behind a preacher's words, or the pathos beneath someone's prayer? A community where you are known and loved anyway, across years and shared experiences, filled with mistakes but also victories? The joy of the gospel message that claims *even you* as beloved, and redeemed, and whole?

Years before I became a pastor, I led the missions committee at the comfortable, suburban church I attended with my family. As a committee chair, I had a mailbox at the church office, and one day it held a handwritten letter from a woman named Jamie who was asking us to pick her up and get her to church. She was confined to a wheelchair and the bus system for disabled persons didn't run on Sundays. She used to attend a United Methodist church in her hometown in north central Iowa. She was living in Des Moines now and really wanted to have church in her life.

I read the letter without enthusiasm and then left it in my mailbox for several weeks.

We didn't have a church bus. Jamie didn't live in our neighborhood. Her letter felt like an unwelcome nuisance.

But I didn't throw it away.

Jamie had explained in the letter that she was writing to several churches. I waited to respond, leaving ample time for other churches to act. But that letter sat there with its silent reproach every time I checked my mailbox. When it seemed a suitable period had passed for other churches to seize this opportunity, I reluctantly called the phone number in the letter.

Yes, Jamie was still looking for a church. No, none of the other churches had responded. Sure, she'd love for me to come and meet her.

I later learned that Jamie sent her letter to two dozen churches. No one responded, until I did. I made my friend Barb go with me when I went to Jamie's apartment. I didn't know what I was getting myself into, and I needed reinforcements.

Jamie turned out to be a lovely young woman who had been confined to a wheelchair from a very young age with cerebral palsy. She was small and funny, and none of our questions were off limits. She educated us on the limitations of the bus schedule, and about how she would manage the bathroom if she were to come to our church, and how someone might get her into a car and manage her wheelchair. Out of that conversation grew a ministry we called "Wheels," in which members of a team of volunteers signed up to go to Jamie's apartment week by week, pick her up, bring her to church, and take her home again afterward. Every one of those families enjoyed spending time with Jamie, and there was joy as she became a familiar face in our midst.

It didn't occur to me back then to ask Jamie what she saw in the church, or why she wanted to come there. A lifelong church member myself, that was never the first question on my mind. Looking back, though, I find myself curious: Why did she make such extraordinary efforts to get to church? It was no small task. Why was it so important to her?

I used to worry when staunch members of Women at the Well would leave. Each week we invite those to come forward who are leaving prison in the coming week so that we can "pray them out," with everyone in the room raising hands in their direction. Sometimes I don't know the women who are leaving; a friend encourages them to come for that prayer, or they've never paused long enough for a conversation. But sometimes those women are very dear to me.

One evening five beloved sisters stood before me at the end of the worship service, excited to be prayed out. Each one of them was a nearly-every-week attender, and I had come to know them in various ways, through our leadership group, our choir, baptism, pastoral care, or our reentry program. My voice caught as I prayed over them—not just because I would miss them, but also from that jolt of unease that we, as a church, would be weakened by their departure.

Over time I have learned that the grief is real, but I don't need to worry. We have prayed out countless women whose presence enriched and enlivened Women at the Well during their stay of months or years. But our prison releases and admits about 10 percent of our population *every month*. That means we are welcoming between sixty-five and ninety women into the institution every thirty days, and when one seat is left empty in our worship space, it seems someone new will always fill it. Some of these women will become strong, beloved leaders who, when it is their turn to be prayed out, will also be sorely missed.

Those seats get filled inside the prison in part because we invite. It has been said that the average United Methodist in the US invites someone to church once every thirty-eight years.[2] Inside the prison, I'd say our average attender invites someone every thirty-eight days—or sooner! Friends come with friends. Inviting is made easier when new friends are always at hand.

2. Farr et al., *Get Their Name*, 21.

I once asked our inside leaders the *why* question: Why do you come to church? Why do you invite others? Kelli answered, without hesitation, "Because I want to be a different person." Ginni spoke of peace, and being reminded of what's important in life, and then said, "It makes me feel like I can breathe again." Others mentioned learning, hearing the word God has for them, religious and spiritual growth, and fellowship. "I come to be with like-minded people." "This is my family."

The energy I hope you hear in these answers is felt in our worship service week by week. Each Thursday, as worship begins, I stand before this unlikely gathering and smile at those assembled friends, sisters, and strangers. I spread my arms wide and say, "God is good." "All the time," comes the response, with an energy larger than the number and circumstances of the women gathered there. "All the time," I continue, looking out with love and welcome for these rows of women—some of whom I know are facing horrendous hurts and challenges. Their response astonishes me in its reckless truth for them and for us all: "God is good!"

I wonder whether we average church people, out in the world, know that truth. In my experience, we don't come to church with a lot of clarity over why we're there, nor can we always articulate why it might make a difference to someone else. In the business world, we are encouraged to have an "elevator speech"—a summary of what we're about—that we could convey in the thirty seconds it takes to go up or down an elevator. Adam Hamilton says we church folks ought to be clear about the answers to three questions: "1. Why do people need Christ? 2. Why do people need the church? 3. Why do people need *this particular* church?"[3] I suspect that many of us don't have answers to those questions that we could voice succinctly.

Church has always been important to me, but I haven't always had words to explain that to someone else. In the years before I was a pastor, I regularly attended choir practice on Wednesday nights and, later, praise band practice on Saturday mornings. But if a colleague pressed me to be at the office during those times, I almost never told them the reason behind my "no." I'd say, "I have another commitment." To name the joy and loyalty I felt for these activities felt impossible; singing songs of praise to God seemed a little quaint, somehow inconsistent with my carefully curated image as a serious professional. For a lot of years, I wasn't ready or able to explain why my faith mattered.

3. Hamilton, *Leading Beyond the Walls*, chapter 2.

If we can't answer questions like that, we're likely to be pretty lackadaisical about inviting others. We might even buy into the cultural norm that increasingly says, "to each her own." I'm as open as the next (progressive) Christian to persons who hold to different religious persuasions, but I no longer think silence is an adequate response when someone says she's given up on church, or that she can't believe in God any more. I want to be ready to ask why, to really listen to her story, and perhaps to explain why I *still* go to church, and how the God I know still commands my devotion. If we who are faithful Christians aren't ready to claim those truths, in words, face to face with people we know, who will?

It's a real question in a culture that doesn't really know Jesus anymore. Young people increasingly do not think of the United States as a Christian nation, or give Christian identity any kind of deference.[4] The words that began this chapter—that The Church has something critically important to offer—would not compute for many people in our communities. The media portray us as a caricature of our greater purposes, less as a people of love and justice and more as folks marked by infighting, judgment, exclusion, money-grubbing, political-power-mongering, and a spirituality disconnected from real life.

As a result, when a community has a problem it needs to solve, its churches no longer surface as helpful partners in that work. It's partly because the people in agencies, nonprofits, and elected offices locally and nationally are no longer, many of them, churched people themselves. They aren't so likely to think of us, nor know how to connect with us, when they want to effect change in the community. Those efforts go forward, and they succeed or fail, without our involvement. And so it becomes a downward spiral: we don't make a good case for why our churches matter, and so we attract fewer people, and have a smaller reach, so fewer people expect much of us, and our work for good in the world is reduced, and so on until it's hard to talk about what we are doing there in the first place.

And the answer we used to give, as we hurried off to a church function—"I have another commitment"—begins to shift to—"I guess I can cancel that thing I was going to do tonight."

When I served as pastor to a church outside the prison for eight years, I knew it mattered that I was there. I had important conversations with people who were hurting. We offered beautiful and vital worship, week

4. Winston, "'Christian America' Dwindling."

after week, and the church grew to the point that we needed two worship services, which meant even more beautiful and vital worship, in different styles, incorporating the talents of many more persons. I wrote a weekly blog, and we did some great missions together, and we empowered laypersons to be teachers and leaders in many worthy ministries. I am proud of the work I did in that church.

But soon after I arrived in prison, I noticed a basic difference in these ministry settings. *At the prison,* I have the sense *every day* that it matters that I'm there. It matters because I have conversations with women who are openly facing the hardest challenges of their lives. They wonder whether there is anyone who cares, and if there is a way forward. I get to offer the dignity of a reply to every message I receive, in a setting where too many questions go unanswered. I try to learn her name, and use it, and help her know that she is beloved.

In the last week, at the time of this writing, I helped bring Vacation Bible School to our adult residents—three nights of music, crafts, games, and Bible study that brought joy and energy to more than 1/10 of our residents. I had a heartfelt conversation with Kirstyn who is back in prison and needed to talk through where God wants her to go next, and whether God could be with her if she has to go to a state-run facility rather than to her home ("God can," I said!), and what can she work on while she waits to be released? Lindsay came to my office in the midst of mania and despair, pouring out a life story of rape, torture, incest, humiliation, mental illness, suicide attempts, and the death of more than one caregiver. Her tears and frenzy slowed as our conversation turned to her hope for the future, and the person she cares for, and hopes to marry. I spoke with Makayla about her deep indecision about whether to go forward with baptism and with Molly about why she did not connect with the reentry team with which we had matched her. I baptized five women, and five more reaffirmed their baptism in a worship service filled with joy and tears (including mine). This was perhaps a particularly full week, but every week holds its own riches. It matters that I'm there, every day.[5]

––––––––

5. In many churches, many of these tasks would be carried out by teams of laypersons, or by other staff members. Whether or not we have the direct contacts that I describe, it can matter significantly that we are there to do that empowering.

In the glow of those stories, I am ashamed to tell you the rest of the story of Jamie, the woman we helped through the Wheels ministry I led years ago.

Jamie soon became a beloved member of our community. She told me, well after the fact, that those rides to the church soon included regular lunches and even afternoon activities with the families of her drivers. We as a church were rather proud to have taken on this needful work of helping her join us. After awhile, she started dating a man who was blind. She called me to ask if the Wheels folks could pick him up, too, so he could join her at church. He didn't live far from her, so I put it to our volunteers, and pretty soon this man had been added to their route. Now we had these two people being served by our Wheels ministry.

Then one day Jamie called me and she said, "I have this other friend." The friend was also in a wheelchair, and she had heard about Wheels, and she wanted Jamie to ask if we'd pick her up, too.

The truth is, this was not a surprise. Somewhere in those months that Jamie had been coming to church, I had thought to myself, "Wow, there must be a whole underserved population of women and men, like Jamie, who would love to have a way to get to church." It had never occurred to me to wonder why there weren't wheelchair-bound persons in the congregation. Having learned that buses didn't run on Sundays, I found myself imagining a whole new ministry to fill this gap.

I quailed a bit at that thought. "Omigosh, that could be a lot of work."

Then, immediately, I saw in my mind's eye our sanctuary, filled with wheelchairs and hurting, maimed people, sitting right in our midst like they belonged there. We would be transformed from the comfortable, lovely church that we enjoyed, and we would become *the wheelchair church*.

And then I saw my friends pointing at me and saying, "This is *your* fault."

I'm not proud of any of this, by the way. I'm just trying to tell the truth.

So, I never pursued any further expansion of Wheels. I never even talked about it with anyone. Not with the missions committee. Not with my pastor. At a very deep level, it was a place I wasn't willing to go.

By the time Jamie asked me about her friend who also wanted to come to church, I had already had this conversation with myself. I already had an answer. I said, without any hesitation, "I think the Wheels group is already doing all they can. I don't think we can help anyone else."

Jamie never asked, again, about adding another person. And I never offered.

I didn't have, at that time, the compassion or vision to realize that we as a church had something critically important to offer to Jamie and her friends. That we were meant to be a conduit of the vitally important love and grace God had for them! Jesus would have rejoiced at our sanctuary filled with wheelchairs! I could not. Not then.

I also could not see then that a hearty expansion of our Wheels ministry could have been a gift of critical importance to our church. Important because it would have taught us so much about service, and about being in relationship with other human beings. Important because Jamie and others who did not have a way to join us would have enriched our gathering immensely. Important because it would have been us, being the church we were called to be, growing in love for God and love for our neighbor—and growing especially in mutual love for these new friends God was bringing to us.

All this was way too much foolishness for me, then.

I see that more clearly from inside the prison. I work with dozens of volunteers who join in this work, initially certain that *they* are the ones who have something to offer. Before long each one of us realizes that whatever we bring to this work, we receive much more. We have a role in a bigger work that God is doing at the prison. We have our roles, but there are many roles, and perhaps the most important happen when the women there minister to us and to one another. They know things that we outsiders do not.

Like Connie did, when a woman in the prayer group wept over her addiction, and the way it had taken her away from her children. Connie is a founding member of our congregation and the Tuesday night prayer group called Gap Sisters.[6] This ever-shifting group of sisters literally do stand in the gap for one another. Outside volunteers make this weekly gathering possible, but the group is led by our residents.

That night Erin wept and wondered, "How will I ever forgive myself for choosing drugs over my kids?" The volunteer sat mute as Connie responded wholeheartedly: "Oh, honey, you didn't." Connie paused and smiled knowingly. "You just thought you could have it all."

---

6. This group is named after Ezekiel 22:30.

Connie was right, of course. Right a thousand times over, right in response to so many others who have lived this same anguish. It was a rightness born of Connie's personal experience. She spoke from wisdom born of decades in which she first reproached herself in a similar way, and ultimately found peace in a deeper truth.

Connie built on her own lived experience to respond to the need of a hurting sister. This is the essence of "incarnational ministry": ministry that grows out of one's own immersion in the challenges one seeks to address.[7] The idea of incarnation is most clearly illustrated in Jesus who, although he was in his very nature God, took on human flesh, lived our lives and understands our struggles (Phil 2:5–11). We in turn are "incarnated"—enfleshed—among persons who are hurting and in need of justice when we are immersed in their midst.[8]

It was Connie's incarnational presence with Erin that enabled her to say what others couldn't—like that volunteer, and all of us who do not share that experience. There's a power there greater than well-meaning words spoken by an outsider, which too often feel like mere theory and empty platitudes.

God must long for us as churches to make room for people whose experiences and scars equip them to meet the needs of the overlooked and hidden communities that surround our churches. That includes Erin and Connie, Jamie and her friend to whom I answered *no*, Darlene and Terri, and so many more who are waiting right next door. God must wonder when we will make room for them and then let their experiences become a source of wisdom and solace not just for each other, but for us who have been there all along. We all will be stronger when we learn to make room, and let the intricacies of our many scars be joined into the beauty of life together. We will learn from one another how to speak the timeless truth of God's love and grace *into* and not just *around* the hardest moments of people's lives.

---

7. I am indebted to my friend Bill Mefford for his tireless insistence on the principle of incarnational ministry, which has given shape to my understanding of what I've experienced in prison. He shares about this concept in his excellent book, *The Fig Tree Revolution: Unleashing Local Churches into the Mission of Justice*, where he uses the story of Esther and Mordecai to help local churches consider the process and opportunities for meaningful advocacy. "The only cure for detachment and way out of affluent captivity is incarnational relationship among those directly impacted by injustice. Incarnational relationships among those experiencing injustice are mutually transformative and liberational." Mefford, *The Fig Tree Revolution*, 62.

8. Ibid., 58.

It's those hardest moments that haunt me, as I think about what happens when we gather as a church. Will persons facing deep darkness find anything *for* them? Will they meet anyone whose experience seems relevant to their wounds? I worry about the woman who wanders into your church this Sunday, bearing the visible bruises or unseen lacerations of domestic violence. She almost didn't come at all, and she sits down wondering whether your church has anything for her. Same with the teenager who was raped last weekend by the guy she thought was her boyfriend, or her friend's BFF. And the dad whose son just got arrested again, after two hopeful years, mostly clean. Will they hear anything that touches the depths of their pain? What will happen that tells them: "There's a place for you here"? "Whatever is happening with you, you belong in our midst"? Surely we *already* have persons in our churches who know what it is to survive challenges like these.[9] But in most of our churches, there will be no indication that this is true.

Barbara Brown Taylor laments how many churches wield a kind of "full-solar spirituality" that does not deal well with the possibility of darkness coming into a person's life.[10] Persons facing troubles encounter judgment; "the darkness is your own fault, because you do not have enough faith."[11] It's a truth my wheelchair-bound friend Jamie has experienced in many churches through her life. She arrives and people get excited about the possibility of a faith healing that will rid her of that wheelchair for good. When they pray fervently and healing does not happen, they conclude it's *her* fault. Barbara Brown Taylor says she knows that type, but she does not blame them. She realizes that her troubles, similar to Jamie's, perhaps, had "simply exhausted their resources. They could not enter the dark without putting their own faith at risk . . . . They stood where I could still hear them and begged me to come back into the light."[12]

What a shame for us to wrap the amazing truths of God's love, grace and salvation in a staggering brightness that feels too harsh, too blunt to touch the harder, messier things of life. I am reminded of Parker Palmer describing the soul as "a wild animal"[13] that we scare away when

9. Evils like these are said to affect 1 in 4 women and 1 in 7 men. National Domestic Violence Hotline, "Statistics."

10. Taylor, *Learning to Walk in the Dark*, 6–8.

11. Ibid., 8.

12. Ibid.

13. Palmer, *Hidden Wholeness*, 58.

we preach and teach, assert and argue, claim and proclaim, admonish and advise, and generally behave in ways that drive everything original and wild into hiding. Under these conditions, . . . we scare off all the soulful things, like respectful relationships, goodwill, and hope.[14]

The way to see a wild animal, Palmer says, is to "walk quietly into the woods, sit patiently at the base of a tree, breathe with the earth, and fade into our surroundings," and only then might the wild animal that is the soul make an appearance.[15]

You could say that Nicole's soul dared to show up when, one afternoon early in my time at the prison, Nicole blurted out, "I want to follow God, but not if it's God's will that I lose my daughter." We were sitting with a few other women discussing the words that would be said a few days hence when we joined in the ritual of baptism. As we talked about putting "our whole trust in [Jesus'] grace,"[16] Nicole expressed, more clearly than most of us might, those limits on her willingness to do that.

I knew before that day that Nicole was facing an excruciating situation. Her young daughter was in the care of Nicole's aging relative, who had just announced that this little girl would need to find a different caretaker. Nicole soon realized she had no viable options. The Department of Human Services was involved, and the foster care system. Nicole was facing the real possibility of losing her parental rights to her precious daughter, and she was heartbroken.

In that pre-baptism meeting, in the wake of Nicole's bold words—"I want to follow God, but not if it's God's will that I lose my daughter!"—I found I had nothing to say. All that came to mind were trite words like, "but that's what we're called to do" or "sometimes God knows better than we do." But with Nicole having spoken her truth so plainly, anything I could say would defile this holy moment.

I was surprised when another woman in the circle spoke. With amazing gentleness, Diamond said, "It's what you have to do." We all turned to her, and she went on: "If it's God's will, you'll get through it." Then a sadness crossed her face as she said, "I know. I lost my parental rights to

---

14. Ibid., 59.
15. Ibid.
16. See the baptismal ritual reproduced at appendix 2.

my daughter. It was the hardest thing I've ever done. But I can see she has amazing care and she's in a good place. God knew what she needed."

It was an agonizing wound, and Diamond could speak what I could not. Her words came from her own experience and wisdom in a way that did not sound like pious jabber. This was incarnational ministry, at its best. Her words did not make it all right for Nicole. But they expressed a deep truth: that it is possible to go through such a loss and still be standing, faithful, and hopeful. It was a lesson for me in the immeasurable power of The Church where God arranges us to be present with one another, in the fullness of who we are, with wisdom and experience born of our deepest stories.

Our deepest stories seem to emerge most freely when others make welcoming space for them. Author and pastor Elaine Heath tells of a Sunday when she, a survivor, preached a sermon that addressed childhood sexual abuse—a subject seldom mentioned in church.[17] Afterward a woman nearly eighty years old hung back until they were alone. Soon this woman, Laura, spoke of the rape she had suffered at the hands of two teenaged boys when she was seven years old. Laura had attended church faithfully through all those intervening decades but, she said, "I've never told anyone before."[18] Heath noted the change that came over this woman and her husband in the weeks and months that followed. Where they had previously stayed on the sidelines, it was as if Laura and her husband were set free to enter fully into the life of the community.[19] Laura later explained that she had always wanted to understand the Bible and to know God, but that "was not possible until she heard her own story of suffering within the biblical text. . . . She had to experience the gospel interpreted by a survivor."[20]

My friend Dr. Harold Dean Trulear speaks in numerous churches each year on behalf of his nonprofit called Healing Communities, painting a vision of local congregations serving as "Stations of Hope" for persons affected by the criminal justice system.[21] I've heard him describe his visits to churches where, when he arrives, few will admit they know anyone in prison. He will lead a half-day conversation that breaks the silence on

17. Heath, *We Were the Least of These*, 1–2.

18. Ibid., 3.

19. Ibid.

20. Ibid., 4.

21. Learn more at the Healing Communities website, http://www.healingcommunitiesusa.com/.

this subject, and then on Sunday morning his fiery sermon ends with an altar call. Trulear consistently sees large numbers of congregants come forward—and sometimes their pastor as well!—finally ready to admit what has been true but hidden within that church: nearly everyone is affected by incarceration. It just wasn't safe to talk about it until now.

These experiences of churches becoming places where the hardest wounds can be spoken are repeated with other challenges. Sarah Griffith Lund offers her testimony with respect to mental illness, and invites churches to develop a mental health ministry that includes persons ready to "come out" within the church.[22] Churches develop worship services and other connections for persons suffering with addiction, and a challenge once relegated to AA meetings in back hallways becomes more fully a part of the life of that congregation.[23] As we embrace these possibilities and make space for these challenges to be spoken, it will be *more* true than it already is, that our churches have something critically important to offer the world. We have been impoverished by the absence of people and by the suppression of experiences that, when admitted and valued, will make the church more fully the rich and diverse community that we were always meant to be, more fully the body of Christ. God surely longs to work through us in this way.

To take this idea to what may feel like an extreme, I'll share an idea I heard from a male sex offender who was then incarcerated in Ohio. He offered his vision of a church that would mentor men like him. This happened in a multi-day conversation inside the men's prison in Chillicothe that included more than a dozen residents and as many outside representatives, like me, of prison ministries around the country. One resident had talked about how church folk would shun men like him, when they were out on the streets, in part because they didn't know what to say. Another resident I'll call Clint articulated the "payoff" the church would receive if it enlisted the help of men like him. "One of us who's been there? We'd know

22. Lund, *Blessed Are the Crazy*, appendix; see also Swinton, *Resurrecting the Person*, 156–63 (offering an unflinching case study of one church's support for and friendship with a man affected by mental illness).

23. I'll admit I worry a bit that churches offering these recovery services and programs run the risk of conveying the message that *our main worship services and our committees and programs aren't really the place for you.* While I'm glad for persons in recovery to have the option to gather separately with persons similarly situated, I hope for a "both-and" answer in which a recovering addict is welcomed not just within these special programs, but fully within the life of the church, if she so chooses.

what to say. And we'd bring those people in." Clint went on: "Once you've got a strong foundation in your church, with some sex offenders and some drug addicts and some murderers, then we can begin to have those real conversations in your churches. You give us some space, and once we get on our feet, we can give back."

He said all of this with utter earnestness, without the least bit of irony.[24]

We might be startled—horrified, even—by the foolishness of this vision. Saying *yes* to it would require a "revolution of tenderness," to use the words of Pope Francis.[25] Like Jesus' own incarnation,

> this Christian ideal will always be a summons to overcome . . . all the defensive attitudes which today's world imposes on us. . . . The Gospel tells us constantly to run the risk of a face-to-face encounter with others, with their physical presence which challenges us, with their pain and their pleas, with their joy which infects us in our close and continuous interaction.[26]

Close and continuous interaction with ex-offenders and drug addicts and murderers? In *my* church? There might be an infection there, but is it one of joy? All this may be unsettling, but it's a vision that demands our prayerful attention. It highlights the imperative of the good boundaries, excellent communication, and careful community-building that we have explored in this book. And, wow, what couldn't God do through a church foolish enough to be thrown open in that way? I'm pretty certain Jesus would be in *that* place, with *those* people, having *those conversations*.

Clint's vision makes opening the church to a bunch of people in wheelchairs sound positively tame, doesn't it?!

Our churches make space for incarnational ministry with, by, and through people longing for what The Church in its fullness has to offer.

So how do we become churches that know they have something critically important to offer?

---

24. Portions of this Chillicothe story were first published at Schott, "'Show Us the Church Is for Real.'"

25. Francis, *Joy of the Gospel*, 46.

26. Ibid., 46–47.

We practice what we talked about in this book. I'll admit: The faith community that is only neat and comfortable and timid may not, in fact, have something critically important to offer the world. But we have talked about some core principles that are characteristics of The Church. The Church allows people to bare their scars, and real relationship emerges out of knowing one another, first and foremost. The Church listens, believes, and protects, even when she cannot tell the whole truth or act in accordance with her best interests. The Church welcomes freely but establishes fair and necessary boundaries that help each person to thrive in community. And when something goes wrong, The Church names that and seeks accountability, healing, and reconciliation.

As we take these steps, we will see more clearly the crucial differences between our churches and the other organizations and gatherings that exist in the world. This is a radical welcome that we're talking about here. This is caring that pushes past what politeness and civility require. It moves into *love*—a quality that is ever new in our life together.

We and our churches should be asking whether these things are true of us. *Do* we have something to offer, as we are now? If we cannot answer "yes" with clarity and energy, then we *must* ask, how do we make the changes necessary to get there?

We make room for persons to minister out of their lived experience. When I meet with women getting ready for baptism, we talk about those words in our ritual that ask whether we will "serve as Christ's representatives in the world."[27] I push them a bit, reminding them that, after they stand up and answer these questions of baptism, both friends and foes will be watching them to see what a Christian looks like. It's a daunting prospect, especially in a setting where they don't get to pull themselves together in private before searching and often skeptical eyes will be upon them.

I remind them, though, that these words have a flip side that is positively beautiful. *We get to serve as Christ's representatives in the world!* We probably wouldn't—any of us!—meet the list of qualifications we would enumerate, if it were up to us to tell God who could serve as a worthy representative. Yet God chooses to work through each one of us to further God's purposes in the world. And each one of us is uniquely suited to particular work that only we can take. Because of who we are, where we've been, what

---

27. United Methodist baptismal ritual, portions of which are reprinted at appendix 2.

we notice, and whom we know, we may be the only person who can do what God needs done at this particular moment. What joy, when we get to pursue that work of incarnational ministry, out of the fullness of who we are and what has happened to us. Perhaps we will find ourselves ministering to someone and suddenly know, as a friend says she once realized, that this is the moment for which we were created!

Work for the good of others will always be more insightful, more right, when it comes out of experiences we have lived. Grants are given more often to organizations that include, among their leaders, persons who have experienced the need the organization seeks to meet. Programs are more effective when they are designed by people who have lived the experience that participants are having. The idea of "lived experience" seeks to draw on firsthand accounts and impressions of living through something.[28] Returning citizens often say it this way: "Don't talk about us, without us."

This is an important goal for ministry of all kinds, no matter what kind of work we seek to do in the world. If it is not coming out of someone's lived experience, it is probably generated by an outsider's idea of what would be helpful to "those people."[29] This is a hazard I have had to fight even in the writing of this book. I have spent seven years working at the prison, but I have never been *in prison*. I share this book and its many stories conscious that it is *my* discernment based on experiences that are not fully mine. Having laid this groundwork, I am hopeful that future work (mine and others) may more fully amplify voices that can tell ever more personal truth. In that way we will make room for their incarnational ministry, ever more fully.

We remember that people are hungry. I heard the story of a small church—which may be apocryphal—where worship was interrupted one Sunday morning by a timid knock, soon repeated, on the outer door that opened right into the sanctuary. An usher opened the door to find two young girls standing there, thin and disheveled. "Is this the church that feeds people?" the older girl asked. "No," said the usher, towering over the girls. "That would be the church down the street," motioning to the church

---

28. This article about suicide prevention highlights, for instance, the importance of lived experience among persons offering suicide intervention. Suicide Prevention Resource Center, "Engaging People with Lived Experience."

29. Lupton, *Toxic Charity*, esp. chapter 9; Corbett and Fikkert, *When Helping Hurts*, 106–15.

> *Indeed, the body does not consist of one member but of many.*
> *If the foot would say, "Because I am not a hand, I do not belong*
> *to the body," that would not make it any less a part of the body*
> *. . . If the whole body were an eye, where would the hearing be?*
> *If the whole body were hearing, where would the sense of smell*
> *be? But as it is, God arranged the members in the body, each*
> *one of them, as he chose.* (1 Cor 12:14–15, 17–18)

The Apostle Paul used the image of a human body to illustrate the nature of the church. We were never intended to be all alike; the multiplicity of parts is necessary in order for the body to work properly. We need hand and foot, eye and ear, elbow and pelvis and breast. To lose any one of our parts would mean diminishment.

Just so the church. We are arranged with a diversity of roles and gifts, and if one part is missing, the whole is impoverished. This illustrates the consequences when some sisters and brothers are cut off, either by our unwelcome or their sense that there's nothing for them here. We need one another! We are more whole when we are in this together.

that held the food pantry. The girls backed away, the doors were closed, and worship proceeded.

Surely you agree: *That was the wrong answer.* We are all, always, the church that feeds people! If we are a church at all, there is only one right answer to a question like that. It's *Yes. Come in, dear ones. We're here for you.*

It helps if we remember that all the people we meet are hungry. If they aren't hungry for food and basic human needs, they're hungry for things like meaning, and purpose, for truth and beauty, for connection and peace, and the good news of the gospel of Jesus Christ. Whether it's a person who first comes to our church this weekend or it's the one who has stopped coming, I hope we can pause to discover what that hunger is.

They won't always show it. We all do a pretty good job of acting self-sufficient and self-satisfied. We have been rewarded for that in life! But we The Church must not be fooled. The hunger swells all around us, in our homes, neighborhoods, communities, and nation. The world needs us to respond to that hunger every bit as much as we need the world to expect us to. I pray that our churches understand this, and minister with confidence, trusting that the gospel message of healing, saving, reconciliation, and peace feeds souls today as in ages past, and into an expanding future.

Questions:

a. Describe some ways your church has begun doing ministry out of the personal experiences of your people. In what ways do you find lived experience an important driver of effective ministry? How do those observations differ from ministries we discussed in chapter 2, where "we" do things for "those people" whom we do not know?

b. Does your church have a clear sense that it has something important to offer the world? What is it that you offer? How would a stranger who comes into your church know that?

c. Do you have a story of how your life, personally, has been changed by Jesus Christ, and by the ministry of the church? How many people know your story? Where could you begin telling it? What kinds of incarnational ministry and care might be birthed among you and others whose stories are similar to yours?

d. How is a church strengthened by authentic relationships among people who find the church a safe space for sharing their stories and the wisdom they've gained in overcoming challenging circumstances? What values do we express when we do ministry out of our lived experiences?

e. Take some time to clarify in your own mind what your church has to offer to people who most need community and hope. (Make sure it's true.) Practice explaining that—in less than sixty seconds—to a friend or two, and work on making it compelling. Identify one or two people (or six!) whom you will invite to come to a worship service or other church event, using what you discerned about what your church has to offer. Keep practicing, and honing what you offer, and help others in your church to do the same.

Conclusion

A Community of Love and Forgiveness

we pray, for the wounded ones, knowing that some of us are wounded
and we pray, for the regretful ones, knowing that some of us are regretful
all our hearts and minds are leaning in with clear intention
joining in your way of healing in the world

we pray for the starving ones, knowing that some of us are starving
and we pray for the imprisoned ones, knowing that some of us are imprisoned
all our hearts and minds are leaning in with clear intention
joining in your way of justice in the world

—CHRISTOPHER GRUNDY[1]

By the time they meet me in prison, many women are thirsty for baptism. Having met Jesus, or begun praying again after a long absence, they have found new hope and energy in their practice of faith. We offer baptism several times a year and we have had as many as twenty-one women standing before God and everyone, arrayed across the front of our worship space, ready to take hold of the gift that God has been holding out to them for their whole lives.

In those baptismal services, among the answers and promises and blessings and water that flow through that ritual, my favorite moment comes in the words the congregation repeats as they welcome these new

---

1. Grundy, "Leaning In."

sisters. The congregation is asked whether they will nurture these persons in their Christian life. This is the response we say together:

> With God's help we will proclaim the good news
> and live according to the example of Christ.
> We will surround these persons
> with *a community of love and forgiveness*,
> that they may grow in their trust of God,
> and be found faithful in their service to others.
> We will pray for them,
> that they may be true disciples
> who walk in the way that leads to life.[2]

Nearly every time we say these words, before their echo has died away, I'll pause and ask the congregation, "Do you know what you just said? You promised to surround these friends with 'a community of love and forgiveness.' Are you up to it?"

Being a community of love and forgiveness: That's a staggering promise, no matter where it's made. It's foolishness! It's no easy thing— anywhere—to live up to a promise to be in community with other human beings. Let alone to be a community characterized by love. Plus to yield to the impractical gospel imperative of *forgiveness*. How can a person even dare to speak words like these? They require caution. This is ground even angels must fear to tread!

Not to mention that we make that promise on behalf of *the whole church*. When the people in any particular sanctuary say those words, it's a promise that binds all of us who comprise the church in every time and place.[3] We Christians *all* are part of any congregation's promises, no matter who stands there facing God and the rest of us, claiming her place in God's purposes, and no matter how large or small the gathering that witnesses the rite. We welcome this person into The Church, and it promises to be there for her.

I didn't hear these words with such gravity until I felt them reverberating against our unadorned, pale walls and drifting out our high windows

---

2. From United Methodist baptismal liturgy, reproduced in relevant part at appendix 2 (emphasis mine).

3. I am reminded here of the "Mystical Communion" Avery Dulles describes in chapter 3 of his *Models of the Church*, which emphasizes "the mystical and invisible communion that binds together all those who are enlivened by the grace of Christ. Augustine speaks of a Church that includes not only the earthly but the heavenly." Dulles, *Models*, 43.

past fences topped with razor wire. These words—"a community of love and forgiveness"—are hard anywhere. But here? In a place no one chooses to be, and as messy and raw a place as you'll ever find? Is such a thing even to be imagined?

How unsettling, to put such a promise into words. And what a compelling description of who we mean to be, who God calls us to be, and who we find ourselves becoming, to our immense surprise. *A community of love and forgiveness.*

May it be so.

Appendix 1

About Prison Congregations

Prison Congregations of America (PCA) is a non-profit ministry that helps to plant denominationally sponsored congregations in prisons around the United States. While no two congregations are exactly alike, what they have in common has come to be known as the PCA Model of Prison Ministry:

- The congregation is made up of prison inmates, with "membership" usually defined by participation.

- The congregation is served by a pastor who is trained by and accountable to the sponsoring denomination. This assures accountability and succession.

- The congregation is denominational in governance and support but ecumenical in spirit and practice, open to all residents and staff regardless of race, culture, sexual orientation, and faith tradition. Sacraments are typically open to all who wish to participate.

- The congregation encourages the involvement of inmates in worship, study, and mission projects.

- The congregation is a partnership between the inside congregation and an outside network of supporting churches and community members, which provide prayer support, visitors, volunteers, and financial support.

A prison congregation is not:

- an effort to proselytize inmates from one faith group to another. Any inmate who is eligible and chooses to participate can be involved.

- a replacement for chaplains. The job descriptions are different. The prison pastor's responsibility is to minister to and develop his or her congregation.

For more information, or to further explore this model of ministry, visit PCA's website at www.prisoncongregations.org.

Appendix 2

Selected Portions of the United Methodist Baptismal Liturgy

Introduction to the Service

Brothers and sisters in Christ:
Through the Sacrament of Baptism
    we are initiated into Christ's holy Church.
We are incorporated into God's mighty acts of salvation
    and given new birth through water and the Spirit.
All this is God's gift, offered to us without price.
Through confirmation,
and through the reaffirmation of our faith,
we renew the covenant declared at our baptism,
acknowledge what God is doing for us, and affirm our commitment to
    Christ's holy Church.

Presentation of Candidates

Renunciation of Sin and Profession of Faith

The pastor addresses candidates who can answer for themselves:

On behalf of the whole Church, I ask you:
Do you renounce the spiritual forces of wickedness,

reject the evil powers of this world,
and repent of your sin?

I do.

Do you accept the freedom and power God gives you
to resist evil, injustice, and oppression
in whatever forms they present themselves?

I do.

Do you confess Jesus Christ as your Savior,
put your whole trust in his grace,
and promise to serve him as your Lord,
in union with the Church which Christ has opened
to people of all ages, nations, and races?

I do.

According to the grace given to you,
will you remain faithful members of Christ's holy Church
and serve as Christ's representatives in the world?

I will.

The pastor addresses the congregation, and the congregation responds:

Do you, as Christ's body, the Church,
reaffirm both your rejection of sin
and your commitment to Christ?

We do.

Will you nurture one another in the Christian faith and life
and include these persons now before you in your care?

**With God's help we will proclaim the good news
and live according to the example of Christ.**

We will surround these persons
>   **with a community of love and forgiveness,**
>   **that they may grow in their trust of God,**
>   **and be found faithful in their service to others.**

We will pray for them,
>   **that they may be true disciples**
>   **who walk in the way that leads to life.**

This is followed by a recitation of the Apostles' Creed, the Thanksgiving over the Water, the Baptism with Laying On of Hands, the Reaffirmation of Faith, Reception into the United Methodist Church, Reception into the Local Congregation, and the Commendation and Welcome. The full ritual can be found at https://www.umcdiscipleship.org/resources/the-baptismal-covenant-i.

Appendix 3

Sample Covenant with Sex Offender (and Other Returning Citizens) Coming into the Local Church

This sample form is intended as only a starting point for your use, and it must be tailored to fit your congregation's specific needs. Its inclusion here does not constitute legal or professional advice. You are advised to seek counsel from legal and/or judicatory professionals in your local setting before putting a form of this agreement into place.

Covenant of Participation and Relationship

In the spirit of community, accountability, hospitality, and good mutual communication, [Congregation] (the "Church") and [Returning Citizen] ("you") covenant together as follows:

1. The Church will endeavor to be for you a community of love and forgiveness in which you are welcomed and nurtured to live out and develop your Christian faith.

2. You may attend [specify any permissions and/or limits on participation in the life of the church, such as:

   - "adult worship services on Saturday evenings at 5:00 p.m."

- "such activities as have been approved in advance by [the Senior Pastor]."

"You will contact the Senior Pastor once each week with your proposed schedule of activities for that week. You understand that approval of that schedule will be at the discretion of the Senior Pastor." [or these decisions could reside with the Church Council or other specified leader(s)

3. You agree not to [specify these agreements, such as:

   - "be present on Church property during any programming for children or youth."

   - "be alone at any time with any child, youth, or vulnerable adult other than your own child(ren) as legally allowed."

   - "use any part of the children's ministry area of the Church [when children are present]."

   - "use any restroom that is not a single occupancy restroom."]

4. Whenever you are present on Church grounds you will be accompanied by an Accountability Partner.

   a. The Church will work with you to identify at least three individuals who will agree to serve in this role. All accountability partners will be required to submit to a background check and will then be approved by [the Senior Pastor] [and the Church Council] [as well as the ___th Judicial District parole office or, if applicable, Sex Offender Treatment Program]. Any person designated as an Accountability Partner will receive and review a copy of this Covenant.

   b. You will cooperate with your Accountability Partners in scheduling and planning your presence on Church grounds.

   c. Upon entering upon Church property, you will use the most direct route from the parking lot to the main entrance to these facilities, not passing through other parts of the buildings.

   d. One or more Accountability Partner(s) will accompany you as you move within the Church grounds. This includes any visits to the restroom, fellowship areas, meeting rooms, etc.

5. [if applicable] You agree and understand that your status as a registered sex offender in the State of _____ and your possible presence at the Church under the terms of this Covenant will be shared with [specify whom: the Church Council? the congregation? prospective new members?]. OR You understand that this covenant will remain on file with the Church and will be available to Church members. This covenant will be shared directly with all Church staff members, and anyone else deemed appropriate by the Senior Pastor.

6. [if applicable] You will avoid all contact with children while you are on church property or at any congregation sponsored event. If a child in the congregation approaches you, either at church or elsewhere, you will politely and immediately excuse yourself.

7. Upon request of the Pastor, you shall promptly meet with the Pastor and/or the Church Council regarding your adherence to these guidelines.

8. [if applicable] You will obtain approval from your parole officer and provide proof thereof for the Church participation contemplated under this Covenant.

9. [if applicable] You will continue to participate in a treatment program or counseling group while attending the Church.

10. Subject to the terms of this Covenant, the Church [possibly through leaders as specified] will seek to identify opportunities for you to participate in [adult] activities, ministries, missions, committees, ministry teams, and leadership roles appropriate to your availability, gifts and graces.

11. The Pastor and leaders of the Church will stand behind this Covenant and your participation in the Church under the terms agreed herein, if at any time during its continuation any person having no supervisory authority over you should question your presence and role in the Church.

12. If you should decide to relocate to another congregation, the Pastor or the Church Council may inform one or more leaders of that congregation of the existence and content of this Covenant.

13. It is understood that any conduct which appears to be in violation of State or Federal law or restrictions upon your activities imposed by

any court or parole officer will be reported to the police and/or your parole officer.

14. **You understand that if you violate any terms of this Covenant, you may be immediately denied access to Church functions and property until such violation is resolved. If the violation is not resolved to the satisfaction of the Church, this Covenant may be terminated in the discretion of the Church through its pastor(s), employees or designees, who will have sole discretion to determine whether a violation of this Covenant has occurred. Any such decision will be final upon written communication to you.**

15. The terms of this Covenant may be reviewed at any time at the request of the Church or by you, and will be reviewed with you by [whom] after it has been in effect for [six / twelve / twenty-four] months, with discussion of any appropriate changes based on your progress, or lack thereof, and supervision status.

The parties to this Covenant look forward to growing together as you become a valued friend and the Church is enriched by your presence.

[CHURCH NAME]

_____   _____   _____
Pastor   Chair, Church Council Date

_____   _____
Printed Name:_____   Date

APPENDIX 4

Our Leadership Covenant Based on Jesus' Matthew 18 Process to Address Conflict

Council Membership and Expectations—Women at the Well

1. A person becomes a full member of our Council by attending five scheduled meetings, as follows.

   - These five meetings must be consecutive unless one or more is excused (see paragraph 4 below).

   - If there are excused absences, the candidate must still attend five meetings within a four-month period, unless the Council agrees to extend that period upon explanation.

   - At the fifth meeting, the person's membership will be acted upon by the Council, after discussion among its full members. Council can approve, disapprove, or defer with required action by the candidate.

   - Full members who are released from ICIW and may become full members upon their next return to ICIW by meeting the above requirements with three meetings. They will be considered provisional members from the time they attend their first council meeting until their membership is acted upon by the Council.

2. Until the Council approves a person as a full member, persons working toward full membership are considered "provisional members" who

   - Have voice but not vote on Council business.

   - May—when and if this privilege is restored for council members—remain in the Sacred Place over headcount on Thursday evenings to assist with worship preparation.

   - May NOT participate in Inside/Outside Council meetings.

3. Full members may request a break from Council membership on the following terms:

   - A break shall not be requested within the first year of Council membership, except upon approval by the pastor after conversation with her due to extenuating circumstances.

   - A break shall be for a defined period of up to four weeks per calendar year.

   - During any break, the person shall have the privileges and limitations of a provisional member.

   - At the end of a break, the person shall return to full membership without action by the Council except for addressing any major tickets or other interpersonal concerns that have arisen since the last meeting she attended.

   - A full member who has taken a break may not participate in Inside/Outside Council meetings until she has attended at least two Council meetings.

4. Provisional and full members are expected to

   - Attend all Council meetings and be present at Women at the Well worship on Thursday evenings, unless excused by notifying the pastor (in advance where possible) for

     o Work

     o Illness

     o Room confinement or detention

     o Classes and/or programs

     o Other extenuating circumstances

- When and if this privilege is restored for council members, assist when possible with worship set-up over headcount. It is understood that not all Council members are needed every week during this time. At times when not enough members are attending, the need will be communicated and members will be expected to assist.

5. Full members of council who have three unexcused absences from Council meetings and/or worship in a three-month period will be contacted by a Council member (or by a pastor, if no council member can readily make contact), to find out what is happening and to offer support. At that time the Council may in its discretion (possibly after asking the member to complete some action with respect to her absences) excuse one or more of those absences. Unless the Council takes other action based on an individual's circumstances, upon five unexcused absences from Council meetings and/or worship in any three-month period, the person's membership on the Council will terminate. A member terminated in this way is free to rejoin the Council by starting over as outlined in this document.

6. Council members will hold each other accountable—with discretion and compassion—for Christian behavior inside and outside the Sacred Place. Their behavior on the yard and in their units and work sites should be consistent with their Christian beliefs.

7. Council members will endeavor to use the model Jesus taught in Matthew 18 to resolve disagreements that may arise between us and with others in the church and community. This includes:

   - expressing concerns and negative feelings first to the person that has offended you, not to others;

   - if the issue is not resolved, and if it appears feasible, ask another council member to join in further conversation about the issue with the person who has offended you;

   - if the issue is still not resolved, bring the pastor into the conversation to attempt resolution.

8. In the event that

   - any full or provisional member is found guilty on a major disciplinary ticket; or

- two or more Council members are concerned about the behavior of another full or provisional member, and have previously addressed that concern as outlined in paragraph 7 above but the matter has not been resolved to their satisfaction,

those individuals are expected to share about that situation and respond to questions and concerns from the Council at the next Council meeting she or they attend. At the conclusion of the discussions described in this paragraph, the Council shall decide what steps to take with respect to the situation, including the assignment of some required action, suspending the member's status on the council for up to three months, and/or terminating her Council membership. During any suspension, the person shall have the privileges and limitations of a provisional member.

9. Members of the Council will pray for each other, for the Pastor, and for the congregation.

10. The Council will work to maintain an atmosphere among its members and during its meetings in which Council members (full and provisional) can communicate concerns and honestly express ideas and feelings.

11. Council business will normally be conducted only in scheduled Council meetings. It is understood that when Council members are gathered for other purposes, some questions and matters of Council business may be discussed. Those conversations shall not be considered the action of the Council until and unless confirmed by action of the full Council at a scheduled meeting.

12. Council members (full and provisional) are expected to maintain confidentiality about personal issues and prayer requests shared at meetings. They are encouraged to share the ongoing business decisions made at meetings, but personal issues are to be held confidential, a sacred trust.

A Note on Pronouns

My beloved teacher, Mrs. Buckingham, taught us fourth graders about pronouns. She explained that, when you use a pronoun for a person whose gender you don't know, you must use the male he, or him, or his. Being a good student, I made note of that rule and dutifully applied it (to good marks!), but the fact that I remember that day is evidence of the friction it created in my young spirit. I am reminded of that rule when, with my androgynous name, I receive junk mail addressed to Mr. Lee Schott. A lopsided assumption undergirds this convention: it could never be offensive to a woman to be addressed as a man, but woe to the one who would mistakenly call a man "Ms."

I am increasingly wearied at the androcentric logic that permeates our language. I resisted it in 1988 when, in the essay portion of the Ohio bar exam, I referred to every unspecified character using female pronouns. ("Seriously?" said a male exam-mate. "Are you sure you want them to know you're a woman?") I resist it in worship where we use the gender-inclusive New Revised Standard Version and say, in our weekly communion liturgy, "Blessed is *the one* who comes in the name of the Lord." And I resist it in this book by using "she" whenever an un-gendered character needs a pronoun. Of course this also fits my gynocentric prison work, where many of these stories are birthed. It is my hope that we all might become (as women have had to be for centuries) persons who can see ourselves in one another's stories, even if another gender is used in the telling of it.

Having taken this stand in the writing of this book, I want to acknowledge and thank those who are pressing toward language that is less gendered and binary altogether. As our culture accommodates persons' truth about their gender identity, our previously settled categories must give way. This includes rethinking the binaries of our prison systems that are learning how to accommodate transgender individuals, and churches that have, say, names like *Women* at the Well. This hit home on a rare night recently when we began worship with no male volunteers or guests. I remarked on this thoughtlessly, saying, "We're all women here tonight," and immediately recognized my mistake, as I became aware of at least one resident present who has asked to be addressed as "he." Along with you, I am learning to make this room, too.

Bibliography

Alexander, Michelle. *The New Jim Crow: Mass Incarceration in the Age of Colorblindness.* Rev. ed. New York: New, 2012.

American Civil Liberties Union. "Mass Incarceration." American Civil Liberties Union, Issues. https://www.aclu.org/issues/mass-incarceration#current.

Ashkenazi, Noga. *The Grey Area: Feminism Behind Bars.* WMM (Women Make Movies), 2012. http://www.wmm.com/filmcatalog/pages/c841.shtml.

Avery, Beth. "Ban the Box: U.S. Cities, Counties, and States Adopt Fair Hiring Policies." *National Employment Law Project,* April 20, 2018. http://www.nelp.org/publication/ban-the-box-fair-chance-hiring-state-and-local-guide/.

Banaji, Mahzarin R., and Anthony G. Greenwald. *Blindspot: Hidden Biases of Good People.* New York: Delacorte, 2013.

BBC News. "World Prison Populations." *BBC News.* http://news.bbc.co.uk/2/shared/spl/hi/uk/06/prisons/html/nn2page1.stm.

Blackaby, Henry T., and Claude V. King. *Experiencing God: Knowing and Doing the Will of God.* Nashville: LifeWay, 1990.

Block, Peter, and John McKnight. "Abundant Community: Awakening the Power of Families and Neighborhoods." http://www.abundantcommunity.com/.

Block, Peter, Walter Brueggemann, and John McKnight. *An Other Kingdom: Departing the Consumer Culture.* Hoboken, NJ: Wiley, 2016.

Bolz-Weber, Nadia. *Accidental Saints: Finding God in All the Wrong People.* Colorado Springs: Convergent, 2015.

Brown, Brené. *Rising Strong: The Reckoning. The Rumble. The Revolution.* New York: Spiegel & Grau, 2015.

Bruxvoort Colligan, Richard. "Lament." http://www.worldmaking.net/lament, 2017.

Bruxvoort Colligan, Trish. "Welcome to This Circle." http://www.riversvoice.com/welcome-to-this-circle.php, 1997.

Buel, Sarah M. "Fifty Obstacles to Leaving, a.k.a., Why Abuse Victims Stay." In *The Colorado Lawyer,* 28.10, October 1999, 19–28. http://www.ncdsv.org/images/50_Obstacles.pdf.

Campbell, Justin Scott. "Trauma Makes Weapons of Us All: an interview with adrienne maree brown." *Medium,* May 10, 2018. https://medium.com/@jscottcampbell/trauma-makes-weapons-of-us-all-an-interview-with-adrienne-maree-brown-e6ef7453fd28.

Cleave, Chris. *Little Bee.* New York: Simon & Schuster, 2008.

Bibliography

Cleveland, Christena. *Disunity in Christ: Uncovering the Hidden Forces that Keep Us Apart.* Downers Grove, IL: InterVarsity, 2013.

Cloud, Henry, and John Townsend. *Boundaries: When to Say Yes, How to Say No, to Take Control of Your Life.* Grand Rapids: Zondervan, 1992.

Coates, Ta-Nahesi. *Between the World and Me.* New York: Spiegel & Grau, 2015.

Coogan, Michael D., ed. *The New Oxford Annotated Bible: New Revised Standard Version.* 3rd ed. Oxford: Oxford University Press, 2001.

Corbett, Steve, and Brian Fikkert. *When Helping Hurts: How to Alleviate Poverty without Hurting the Poor . . . and Yourself.* Chicago: Moody, 2012.

Daniel, Lillian. *Tired of Apologizing for a Church I Don't Belong To: Spirituality without Stereotypes, Religion without Ranting.* New York: FaithWords, 2017.

Dickman, Noell. "For Trafficking Victims, Leaving Is Never Easy." *USA Today Network–Wisconsin,* September 18, 2016. https://www.thenorthwestern.com/story/news/2016/09/18/trafficking-victims-leaving-never-easy/90412452/.

Dulles, Avery. *Models of the Church.* Expanded ed. New York: Image, 2002.

Engel, Beverly. "Why Don't Victims of Sexual Harassment Come Forward Sooner?" In *Psychology Today,* November 16, 2017. https://www.psychologytoday.com/us/blog/the-compassion-chronicles/201711/why-dont-victims-sexual-harassment-come-forward-sooner.

Evans, Rachel Held. *Searching for Sunday: Loving, Leaving and Finding the Church.* Nashville: Nelson, 2015.

Farr, Bob, et al. *Get Their Name: Grow Your Church by Building New Relationships.* Nashville: Abingdon, 2013.

Francis, Pope. *The Joy of the Gospel (Evangelii Gaudium).* Apostolic Exhortation. Publication No. 7–458. Washington DC: United States Conference of Catholic Bishops, 2013.

Goode, W. Wilson Sr., Charles E. Lewis, and Harold Dean Trulear. *Ministry with Prisoners and Families: The Way Forward.* Valley Forge, PA: Judson, 2011.

Greenfield, Craig. "The Four Stages of Community: What the Church Can Learn from the Slum." *Craig Greenfield: Creative. World. Justice,* January 15, 2016. http://www.craiggreenfield.com/blog/2016/community.

Gribben, Mark. "Abuser, Lover, Stepfather." *The Malefactor's Register.* http://malefactorsregister.com/wp/abuser-lover-stepfather/.

Groves, Sara. "Like a Lake." On Sara Groves, *Fireflies and Songs.* Sponge Records, 2009.

Grundy, Christopher. "Leaning In: A Prayer of Intention." https://soundcloud.com/christopher-grundy/leaning-in-prayer-of-intention, 2013.

Hall, Mark and Nichole Nordeman. "Stained Glass Masquerade." On Casting Crowns, *Lifesong.* Brentwood, TN: Reunion Records, 2005.

Hamilton, Adam. *Leading Beyond the Walls: Developing Congregations with a Heart for the Unchurched.* Nashville: Abingdon, 2002.

Head, Timothy, and Grover Norquist. "The High Costs of Over-incarceration." *National Review,* August 13, 2015. https://www.nationalreview.com/2015/08/over-incarceration-not-making-america-safer/.

Heath, Elaine A. *We Were the Least of These: Reading the Bible with Survivors of Sexual Abuse.* Grand Rapids: Brazos, 2011.

Human Rights Watch. "US: Sex Offender Laws May Do More Harm Than Good." Human Rights Watch, September 11, 2007. https://www.hrw.org/news/2007/09/11/us-sex-offender-laws-may-do-more-harm-good.

King Center. "The King Philosophy." Atlanta: The King Center. http://www.thekingcenter. org/king-philosophy.

Legal Action Center. *After Prison: Roadblocks to Reentry. A Report on State Legal Barriers Facing People with Criminal Records.* Legal Action Center, 2004. https://lac.org/ roadblocks-to-reentry/upload/lacreport/LAC_PrintReport.pdf.

Lose, David. "Misogyny, Moralism and the Woman at the Well." *Huffpost,* September 19, 2011. https://www.huffingtonpost.com/david-lose/misogyny-moralism-and-the_b _836753.html.

Lund, Sarah Griffith. *Blessed Are the Crazy: Breaking the Silence about Mental Illness, Family, and Church.* St. Louis: Chalice, 2014.

Lupton, Robert D. *Toxic Charity: How Churches and Charities Hurt Those They Help (And How to Reverse It).* New York: HarperOne, 2011.

Malcolm, John G. "The Problem with the Proliferation of Collateral Consequences." *Federalist Society Review* 19, January 29, 2018. https://fedsoc.org/commentary/ publications/the-problem-with-the-proliferation-of-collateral-consequences.

Mann, Alice. *Raising the Roof: The Pastoral-to-Program Size Transition.* Herndon, VA: Alban Institute, 2001.

Mefford, Bill. *The Fig Tree Revolution: Unleashing Local Churches into the Mission of Justice.* Eugene, OR: Cascade, 2017.

Melton, Glennon Doyle. *Love Warrior.* New York: Flatiron, 2016.

Melton, Joy Thornburg. *Safe Sanctuaries: Reducing the Risk of Child Abuse in the Church.* Nashville: Discipleship Resources, 1989.

Mukherjee, Siddhartha. *The Emperor of All Maladies: A Biography of Cancer.* New York: Scribner, 2010.

NAMI (National Alliance on Mental Illness). "StigmaFree." NAMI. https://www.nami. org/stigma.

National Domestic Violence Hotline. "50 Obstacles to Leaving: 1–10." *National Domestic Violence Hotline,* June 10, 2013. http://www.thehotline.org/2013/06/10/50-obstacles-to-leaving-1-10/.

———. "Statistics." *National Domestic Violence Hotline,* Resources. http://www. thehotline.org/resources/statistics/.

O'Leary, Dane. "Addiction and Mental Illness: Does One Cause the Other?" Foundations Recovery Network, Resources & Publications. https://www.dualdiagnosis.org/ addiction-mental-illness-one-cause/.

Palmer, Parker. *An Undivided Life: Seeking Wholeness in Ourselves, Our Work, and Our World.* Louisville, CO: Sounds True Audio, 2009.

———. *A Hidden Wholeness: The Journey Toward an Undivided Life.* San Francisco: Jossey-Bass, 2004.

Pathak, Jay, and Dave Runyon. *The Art of Neighboring: Building Genuine Relationships Right Outside Your Door.* Grand Rapids: Baker, 2012.

Peck, M. Scott. *The Different Drum: Community Making and Peace.* New York: Touchstone, 1987.

Perception Institute. "Implicit Bias." Perception Institute. https://perception.org/research/ implicit-bias/.

Pranis, Kay. *Circle Processes: A New/Old Approach to Peacemaking.* New York: Good Books, 2005.

Putnam, Robert D. *Our Kids: The American Dream in Crisis.* New York: Simon & Schuster, 2015.

Bibliography

Rabuy, Bernadette, and Daniel Kopf. "Prisons of Poverty: Uncovering the Pre-Incarceration Incomes of the Imprisoned." Prison Policy Initiative Reports, July 9, 2015. https://www.prisonpolicy.org/reports/income.html.

Rainer, Thom S., and Eric Geiger. *Simple Church: Returning to God's Process for Making Disciples*. Nashville: B&H, 2006.

RAINN (Rape, Abuse & Incest National Network). "The Criminal Justice System: Statistics; The Vast Majority of Perpetrators Will Not Go to Jail or Prison." RAINN. https://www.rainn.org/statistics/criminal-justice-system.

Reader, Caryn. "Revisiting the Woman at the Well." *Intervarsity: Women in the Academy and Professions*, May 27, 2014. https://thewell.intervarsity.org/focus/revisiting-woman-well.

Roderick, Libby. "How Could Anyone." On Libby Roderick, *How Could Anyone*. Anchorage, AK: Turtle Island Records, 2005.

Rodgers, Grant. "Woman sentenced to life as juvenile paroled to hospice." *USA Today*, December 4, 2013. https://www.usatoday.com/story/news/nation/2013/12/03/iowa-woman-sentenced-to-life-as-juvenile-paroled/3862315/.

Rovner, Josh. "Juvenile Life without Parole: An Overview." The Sentencing Project, Publications, October 13, 2017. https://www.sentencingproject.org/publications/juvenile-life-without-parole/.

Schott, Lee. "'Show Us the Church Is for Real.'" August 13, 2015. http://www.leeschott.com/?p=68.

Schwartzapfel, Beth, and Hannah Levintova. "How Many Innocent People Are in Prison?" *Mother Jones*, December 12, 2011. https://www.motherjones.com/politics/2011/12/innocent-people-us-prisons/.

Shapiro, Arnold, dir. *Scared Straight*. 1978; Golden West Television. Described in Wikipedia's "Scared Straight" entry; https://en.wikipedia.org/wiki/Scared_Straight!.

Simon, Kim. "I Worked in the Domestic Violence Unit of the Police Department, and Learned the Truth of How Our Legal System Treats Victims." *XO Jane*, September 18, 2014. http://www.xojane.com/issues/domestic-violence-unit-police-department.

Sontag, Susan. "Disease as Political Metaphor." *The New York Review of Books*, February 23, 1978. http://www.nybooks.com/articles/1978/02/23/disease-as-political-metaphor/.

Stevenson, Bryan. *Just Mercy: A Story of Justice and Redemption*. New York: Spiegel & Grau, 2015.

Suicide Prevention Resource Center. "Engaging People with Lived Experience." Suicide Prevention Resource Center. https://www.sprc.org/keys-success/lived-experience.

Swinton, John. *Resurrecting the Person: Friendship and the Care of People with Mental Health Problems*. Nashville: Abingdon, 2000.

Taylor, Barbara Brown. *Learning to Walk in the Dark*. New York: HarperCollins, 2014.

Tutu, Desmond M., and Mpho A. Tutu. *The Book of Forgiving: The Fourfold Path for Healing Ourselves and Our World*. New York: HarperOne, 2014.

United Methodist Publishing House. *The United Methodist Book of Worship*. Nashville: United Methodist Publishing House, 1992.

———. *The United Methodist Hymnal: Book of United Methodist Worship*. Nashville: United Methodist Publishing House, 1989.

United States Conference of Catholic Bishops. "When I Call for Help: A Pastoral Response to Domestic Violence Against Women." United States Conference of Catholic Bishops, Issues and Action. http://www.usccb.org/issues-and-action/marriage-and-family/marriage/domestic-violence/when-i-call-for-help.cfm.

Bibliography

Volf, Miroslav. *Exclusion & Embrace: A Theological Exploration of Identity, Otherness and Reconciliation.* Nashville: Abingdon, 1996.

Warren, Rick. *The Purpose-Driven Church: Growth without Compromising Your Message & Mission.* Grand Rapids: Zondervan, 1995.

————. *The Purpose-Driven Life.* Grand Rapids: Zondervan, 2002.

Weisenthal, Joe. "We Love What Warren Buffet Says About Life, Luck, and 'Winning the Ovarian Lottery.'" *Business Insider,* December 10, 2013. http://www.businessinsider.com/warren-buffett-on-the-ovarian-lottery-2013-12

Weiss, Bari. "The Limits of 'Believe All Women.'" Opinion. *The New York Times,* November 28, 2017. https://www.nytimes.com/2017/11/28/opinion/metoo-sexual-harassment-believe-women.html.

Wilson, Jared C. "10 Reasons Why You Should Underprogram Your Church." *For the Church: Gospel-Centered Resources from Midwestern Seminary,* November 9, 2015. https://ftc.co/resource-library/blog-entries/10-reasons-why-you-should-underprogram-your-church.

Winston, Kimberly. "'Christian America' Dwindling, Including White Evangelicals, Study Shows." *Religion News Service,* September 6, 2017. https://religionnews.com/2017/09/06/embargoed-christian-america-dwindling-including-white-evangelicals-study-shows/.

Woodiwiss, Catherine. *'I Believe You': Three Essays for a Broken World.* Sexual Violence & the Church. Sojourners, 2014.

Zehr, Howard. *Changing Lenses: Restorative Justice for Our Times.* 25th anniv. ed. Harrisonburg, VA: Herald, 1990.